Your Space

Student's Book 1

Martyn Hobbs and Julia Starr Keddle

CAMBRIDGE
UNIVERSITY PRESS

CAMBRIDGE UNIVERSITY PRESS
Cambridge, New York, Melbourne, Madrid, Cape Town,
Singapore, São Paulo, Delhi, Tokyo, Mexico City

Cambridge University Press
The Edinburgh Building, Cambridge CB2 8RU, UK

www.cambridge.org
Information on this title: www.cambridge.org/9780521729239

First published 2012

Printed in the United Kingdom at the University Press, Cambridge

A catalogue record for this publication is available from the British Library

ISBN 978-0-521-72923-9 Student's Book, Level 1
ISBN 978-0-521-72924-6 Workbook with Audio CD, Level 1
ISBN 978-0-521-72925-3 Teacher's Book, Level 1
ISBN 978-0-521-72927-7 Class Audio CDs (3), Level 1

Contents

Functions	Skills	
Saying hello		
Telling the time		
Classroom English		
Giving instructions		
Talking about personal information and interests		
Talking about facts	**Reading:** understanding personal information on a webpage	**Pronunciation:** /aɪ/ /ɪ/
Saying where you are from	**Listening:** understanding children talking about their interests	**Study skills:** noticing punctuation
Personal information	**Speaking:** talking about a friend's interests	
Greetings, introductions and saying goodbye	**Writing:** writing a paragraph about yourself for a webpage	
Talking about homes	**Reading:** different kinds of houses	**Pronunciation:** /s/ /z/ /ɪz/
	Listening: children talking about their houses	**Study skills:** vocabulary notebook
	Speaking: describing your ideal house	
Describing a room	**Writing:** writing a paragraph about your ideal house	
Asking for and giving personal information		
Talking about family	**Reading:** answering questions about a poster for a film	
	Listening: family descriptions	
Talking about possessions	**Speaking:** describing a family	
	Writing: answering questions about a film	
Saying when you do things	**Reading:** jobs	**Pronunciation:** sentence stress
	Listening: people talking about their jobs	
Talking about your interests	**Speaking:** guessing your partner's job	**Study skills:** noticing words
Buying a ticket	**Writing:** writing a paragraph about jobs	
Talking about how well you can do something	**Reading:** a summer sports camp	**Pronunciation:** can/can't /ɪŋ/
	Listening: weird animal facts	
	Speaking: sport	
Talking about likes and dislikes	**Writing:** describing free time activities	**Study skills:** making notes
Making suggestions		

Contents

School

Food

Places

The past

The future

Extras

Functions	Skills	
Talking about your daily routine	**Reading:** school clubs	
	Listening: children talking about school routines	
Talking about obligation	**Speaking:** talking about school routine	
Talking about possession	**Writing:** writing an email about your school	
Invitations		
Talking about quantity	**Reading:** school meals	**Pronunciation:** /ɪ/ /iː/
	Listening: children talking about school meals	**Study skills:** word maps
Talking about food	**Speaking:** talking about your favourite food	
Ordering food	**Writing:** writing a food diary	
Talking about actions in progress	**Reading:** an article about Liverpool	**Study skills:** finding key words
	Listening: an article about Liverpool	
Talking about the weather	**Speaking:** describing your town or city	
	Writing: writing about your town or city	
Asking the way and giving directions		
Talking about past events	**Reading:** great travellers	**Pronunciation:** /t/ /d/ /ɪd/
	Listening: great travellers	
Talking about past events	**Speaking:** talking about inventions	
Buying train and bus tickets	**Writing:** writing about where you were	
Talking about the future	**Reading:** great mysteries	
	Listening: explaining mysteries	
Agreeing and disagreeing	**Speaking:** talking about different topics	
Making and suggesting plans	**Writing:** writing about different topics	
Revision		

What's your name?

1 🔘 **1.02** **Listen and read the conversation. Match the names with the photos.**

1 Josh ☐   **2** Poppy ☐   **3** Marek ☐

a    b    c

Poppy's world

A new house. A new friend.

Marek   Hi. I'm Marek. What's your name?
Poppy   My name's Poppy.
Marek   Cool. How old are you Poppy?
Poppy   I'm eleven. And you?
Marek   I'm twelve.
Josh   Hi! My name's Josh.
Marek   Hi, Josh. I'm Marek. Welcome to Avon Road.
Josh   Thanks!

2 🔘 **1.03** **Look at** *Phrasebook*. **Listen and repeat the phrases. Act out the new conversations.**

Phrasebook

What's your name?
My name's ...
How old are you?
I'm eleven.
Cool!
Thanks!

Alphabet

3 🔘 **1.04** **Listen and repeat the alphabet.**

A B C D E F G H I J K L M N O P Q R S T U V W X Y Z

4 **Add the letters of the alphabet to the table.**

Vowels
a e

Consonants
b c d

5 🔘 **1.05** **Listen and write the names.** 1 *Kimura*

6 **Work in pairs. Practise with different names.**
A What's your name?   **B** Justin.
A How do you spell that?   **B** J-U-S-T-I-N.

Everyday words

7 🔊 **1.06** **Match the words with the pictures. Then listen and check.**

a bag ☐   a phone ☐   a watch ☐   a banana ☐   an umbrella ☐
the sun ☐   the moon ☐   a pizza ☐   an apple ☐   an ice cream ☐

1   2   3   4   5

6   7   8   9   10

8 **Copy the words into the correct group.**

a + consonant	**an + vowel**	**the + all letters**
a bag	an umbrella	the sun

9 **Work in pairs. Ask and answer questions about the words.**
A How do you spell apple?   **B** A-P-P-L-E.

Numbers

10 🔊 **1.07** **Listen and repeat the numbers.**

1 one   2 two   3 three   4 four   5 five   6 six   7 seven   8 eight   9 nine   10 ten
11 eleven   12 twelve   13 thirteen   14 fourteen   15 fifteen   16 sixteen   17 seventeen
18 eighteen   19 nineteen   20 twenty   21 twenty-one   30 thirty   31 thirty-one

11 🔊 **1.08** **Listen and write the numbers your hear.**
a ....   b ....   c ....   d ....   e ....   f ....

12 🔊 **1.09** **Listen and complete the telephone numbers.**

a   01488 4 ...... 693 ......   b   055 ...... 10 6   c   0149 ...... 53 ...... 5 0

13 **Work in pairs. Ask and answer these questions.**
• What's your name?   It's …
• How do you spell it?
• What's your telephone number?   It's …
• How old are you?   I'm …

Telling the time

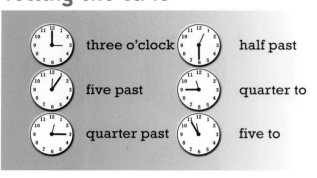

three o'clock

half past

five past

quarter to

quarter past

five to

What's the time?

It's half past twelve.

1 ◉ **1.10** Complete the times. Then listen and repeat.

twenty   seven   ten   five   half   six   quarter

1 It's six o'clock.

2 It's five past six.

3 It's .... past six.

4 It's quarter past ....

5 It's .... past six.

6 It's twenty-five past six.

7 It's .... past six.

8 It's twenty-five to seven.

9 It's twenty to ....

10 It's .... to seven.

11 It's ten to seven.

12 It's .... to seven.

2 ◉ **1.11** Listen and draw the times on the clocks.

1    **2**   **3**   **4**    **5**   **6**

3 Ask and answer times about the clocks in Exercise 2.

A What's the time?   **B** It's ten past eleven.

A It's the weekend. Marek is next door with his new friends.

Marek	Hi, Poppy!
Poppy	Hi, Marek.
Marek	Hello, Mrs Young.
Mrs Young	Hi, Marek. How are you?
Marek	I'm fine, thanks. And you?
Mrs Young	Fine, thanks.
Mr Young	Good morning, Marek.
Marek	Hello, Mr Young.

B

Mrs Young	Poppy!
Poppy	What's the time?
Marek	It's half past twelve.
Poppy	It's lunchtime!

C

Marek	Bye, Poppy. Goodbye, Mrs Young.
Mrs Young	Bye, Marek.

4 Warm up Look at *Poppy's world*. Who is in each photo?

Mr Young   Mrs Young   Marek   Poppy   Josh

Photo 1	
Photo 2	
Photo 3	Marek

5 1.12 Listen and read the photo story. Write the names.

1 Marek 'Hi, Poppy!'
2 _____ 'Hello, Mrs Young.'
3 _____ 'Hi, Marek.'
4 _____ 'Good morning, Marek.'
5 _____ 'Hello, Mr Young.'
6 _____ 'Bye, Poppy.'
7 _____ 'Goodbye, Mrs Young.'
8 _____ 'Bye, Marek.'

6 1.13 Look at *Phrasebook*. Listen and repeat the phrases.

7 Work in pairs. Act out the conversations in *Poppy's world*. Use your own names.

Phrasebook

Hello.   Hi!
Good morning.
Good afternoon.
Good evening.
How are you?
Fine, thanks. And you?
Goodbye.   Bye.
Goodnight.

Classroom English

1 **Warm up** **Match the words with the things in the classroom.**

a desk [12]   a chair ☐   a door ☐   a window ☐   a computer ☐   a board ☐
a poster ☐   a bookcase ☐   a bin ☐   a map ☐   a student ☐   a teacher ☐

◎ 1.14 **Listen and repeat the words.**

2 **Count the things in your classroom. Make a list.**
fifteen desks   three posters   four windows

3 **◎ 1.15** **Listen and match the words with the pictures. Then listen and check.**

1 Open your books. [C]   **3** Write. ☐   **5** Read. ☐   **7** Stand up. ☐
2 Close your books. ☐   **4** Listen. ☐   **6** Sit down. ☐   **8** Put up your hand. ☐

A   B   C   D

E   F   G   H

4 **◎ 1.16** **Listen and follow the teacher's instructions.**

School bags

5 🔊 **1.17** Listen and complete the conversations.

> repeat   understand   speak

A Teacher Anna, open the window.
Student I'm sorry, I don't ....

B Teacher Open your books at page 15.
Student Can you .... that, please?
Teacher Open your books at page 15.

C Teacher Look at the picture. Is there a desk?
Student Can you .... slowly, please?
Teacher Look at the picture. Is there a desk?

6 🔊 **1.18** Match the words and colours. Then listen and check.

orange   red   white   black   pink   brown   purple   green   blue   yellow

7 Match the lists with the school bags. Write the names.

Adam
a pen
a calculator
three pencils
two exercise books

A
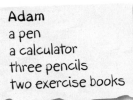
_____

Molly
two books
three pens
four coloured pencils
a ruler
a diary

B

_____

George
an eraser
a calculator
two exercise books
a pen
a pencil case

C

_____

8 🔊 **1.19** Listen and repeat the words.

9 What's in your school bag? Write a list.

10 Work in pairs. Describe your school bag.
A What's in your school bag?
B A pencil case, five exercise books, …
A What colour is your bag?
B It's blue and red.

Days of the week and months of the year

1 🔘 **1.20** **Listen and complete the rap with these words.**

friends   time   hello   goodbye   school   park   books

2 🔘 **1.20** **Match the days of the week with the pictures. Then listen and sing the song.**

Days of the week rap

It's Monday, it's Monday – it's say ¹........................... day,
It's Tuesday, it's Tuesday – it's open your ²........................... day,
It's Wednesday, it's Wednesday – it's late for ³........................... day,
It's Thursday, it's Thursday – it's tell the ⁴........................... day,
It's Friday, it's Friday – it's say ⁵........................... day,
It's Saturday, it's Saturday – it's fun in the ⁶........................... day,
It's Sunday, it's Sunday – it's family and ⁷........................... day.

3 **Work in pairs. What about you? Write the lines of the song for you.**
It's Monday, it's Monday – it's fun in the park day.

4 🔘 **1.21** **Listen and repeat the months.**

January   February   March   April   May   June
July   August   September   October   November   December

5 **Work in pairs. How do you spell the days and months?**
A How do you spell January?   **B** J-A-N-U-A-R-Y.

6 **Work in pairs. Ask and answer.**
A What's your favourite month?
B It's August.

Ordinal numbers

7 🔊 **1.22** **Write the words next to the ordinal numbers. Then listen and repeat.**

ninth	first	fifth	eighth	seventh
fourth	third	second	tenth	sixth

1st *first*	2nd	3rd	4th	5th ....
6th	7th	8th	9th	10th ....

8 🔊 **1.23** **Listen and put the names in the correct positions.**

BOYS
Sam   Thomas
Harry   Callum
Daniel

GIRLS
Sophie Lucy
Olivia Emily
Jessica

boys' names Top 10

1st	Jack
2nd	
3rd	James
4th	Joshua
5th	
6th	
7th	
8th	Joseph
9th	Matthew
10th	

girls' names Top 10

1st	Chloe
2nd	
3rd	Megan
4th	Charlotte
5th	
6th	Lauren
7th	
8th	
9th	Hannah
10th	

9 🔊 **1.24** **Complete the gaps. Then listen and check your answers.**

11th eleven   12th twelfth   13th thirteenth   14th fourteenth   15th fifteenth
16th sixteenth   17th s........teenth   18th e........teenth   19th n........teenth

20th twentieth   21st twenty-first   22nd twenty-second   23rd twenty-t...........

30th thirtieth   31st thirty-...........

10 **Work in groups. Ask and answer questions.**

What's the date?   It's the twenty-first of September.
When's your birthday? And your best friend / mum / dad?   It's on the seventh of April.

Welcome

Interests

1 **Match the words with the pictures.**

sport [2]   animals [ ]   music [ ]   computers [ ]   films [ ]   fashion [ ]   books [ ]   art [ ]

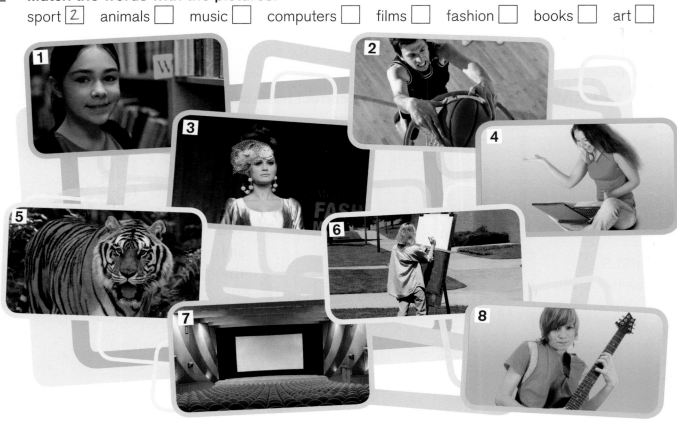

2 🔘 **1.25** **Listen to the students and** (circle) **their interests.**

Martin	Megan	Matthew
animals	music	sport
art	books	art
computers	sport	films

3 **Work in pairs. Ask and answer the question.**

A What are your interests?
B Animals and music. And you?

4 🔘 **1.26** Listen and complete the conversation.

Marek interviews Poppy ...

Marek	What's your name?
Poppy	My name's ¹_____ .
Marek	How old are you?
Poppy	I'm ²_____ .
Marek	When's your birthday?
Poppy	It's on the 21st of June.
Marek	What's your phone number?
Poppy	It's ³_____ .
Marek	Where are you from?
Poppy	I'm from ⁴_____ .
Marek	What are your interests?
Poppy	My interests are ⁵_____ .
Marek	What's your favourite colour?
Poppy	It's ⁶_____ .

Poppy's world

5 Work in pairs. Act out the interview.

6 Complete the Factfile for Poppy.

FACTFILE

Name	Poppy Young
Age	
Birthday	
Phone number	
From	the UK
Interests	
Favourite colour	

7 🔘 **1.27** Complete the Factfile for Marek. Then listen and check.

01584 334287   ~~Marek Adamski~~   red   12
14th May   Poland   computers and sport

FACTFILE

Name	Marek Adamski
Age	
Birthday	
Phone number	
From	
Interests	
Favourite colour	

8 Write the interview with Marek.

9 Complete the Factfile for you.

FACTFILE

Name	
Age	
Birthday	
Phone number	
From	
Interests	
Favourite colour	

10 Work in pairs. Interview your partner.

1A My best friend is Tom

Grammar
subject pronouns • be – positive form • possessive adjectives – singular • regular plurals

Functions
talking about facts • saying where you are from

Presentation

1 **Warm up** Look at the webpage on page 19. Tick (✓) the things you can see.

a mobile phone ☐   a guitar ✓   a football ☐

a computer ☐   a bicycle ☐   a football scarf ☐

2 ◉ **1.28** Read and listen to the webpage. Are the sentences true (*T*) or false (*F*)?

1 Luke is from London. T   **4** Grace is his mum.

2 His parents are from Brazil.   **5** His best friend is Tom.

3 His brother Sam is nine.   **6** Luke is a Chelsea fan.

3 Read *Language focus*. Find the short forms of:

am ...'m...........   is ....   are ....

4 Complete the sentences with *'m*, *'re* or *'s*.

1 I ...'m........... twelve.

2 She .... from San Francisco.

3 He .... in Year 7.

4 We .... in the school band.

5 They .... at school.

6 I .... from Athens.

Language focus

- **I'm** British.
- My sister **is** five.
- My sister**'s** naughty.
- My best friend **is** Tom.
- He**'s** in my class.
- We**'re** Manchester United fans.
- My hobbies **are** music and sport.
- They**'re** in my room.

Vocabulary • Countries

5 ◉ **1.29** Match the countries with the nationalities. Then listen and check.

1 Spain   **2** India   **3** Germany   **4** France   **5** Ireland   **6** Brazil   **7** China   **8** The USA

a French   **b** Brazilian   **c** Irish   **d** Chinese   **e** American   **f** German   **g** Spanish   **h** Indian

6 Work in pairs. Say where the place is. Your partner says the place name.

Brasília   Dublin

Paris   Beijing

New Delhi   Madrid

New York   Berlin

Sam It's a German city.
Leah It's Berlin.
Sam That's right.

Sam It's in Ireland.
Leah It's Madrid.
Sam That's wrong. It's Dublin!

http://yourspace.cambridge.org/

 1.28

About my life

Luke Kelly

Home | **Profile** | Photos

My family

My mum and dad are from Ireland.

My brother Sam is sixteen. His favourite football team is Chelsea.

My sister is five. Her name's Grace. She's naughty!

My friends and hobbies

My best friend is Tom. He's in my class. We're Manchester United fans. His mum and dad are from Poland.

My Manchester United scarf.

My hobbies are music and sport. My favourite things are my guitar and my computer. They're in my room.

About Me

Hi! My name's Luke. I'm British. I'm from London.

Information

Birthday:
12th May

Age:
12

Your space   Talking about you

7 **Complete the sentences about you.**

My name's ¹_____.   My dad is from ⁴_____.
I'm from ²_____.   My mum is from ⁵_____.
I'm ³_____. (age)   My favourite football team is ⁶_____.

8 **Work in pairs. Tell your partner your sentences.**

My name's Claire.

be – positive

1 **Complete the text. Use the tables to help you.**

Hi! I'm Max. ....'m from London.
This is Lara. ....'s from Dublin.
This is Zak. ....'s from New York.

And ..W..e..'re friends!

full form	
I	am
you	are
he	
she	is
it	
we	
you	are
they	

short form	
I	'm
you	're
he	
she	's
it	
we	
you	're
they	

2 **Complete the sentences with *am*, *is* or *are*.**

1 Sam _is_ my best friend.
2 They .... in my class.
3 We .... in class 7D.
4 I .... twelve.
5 He .... from Scotland.
6 Your computer .... old.
7 She .... Spanish.
8 You .... late.

3 ✎ **Complete the form for a friend. Then write sentences.**

Name	
Age	
Nationality	
Class	

His name's Ali and he's eleven. He's Turkish and he's in class 7E.

4 🔘 **1.30** **Read and complete the conversation. Listen and check.**

Arun: Hi. My name'............ Arun.
Gita: And I'............ Gita. We'............ from London.
Arun: She'............ twelve.
Gita: And he'............ twelve, too!
Arun: Our mum and dad .... Indian but we'............ British.

 Get it right!

Use short forms when you speak:
I'm Sofia, what's your name?
NOT ~~I am Sofia, what is your name?~~

5 ○ 1.31 Listen and match.

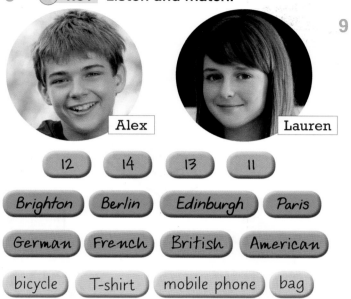

Alex   Lauren

12   14   13   11

Brighton   Berlin   Edinburgh   Paris

German   French   British   American

bicycle   T-shirt   mobile phone   bag

6 ☆ Work in pairs. Invent a new identity. Tell your partner.

Hi, my name's Jake. I'm sixteen ...

Regular plurals

7 Match the singulars with the plurals.

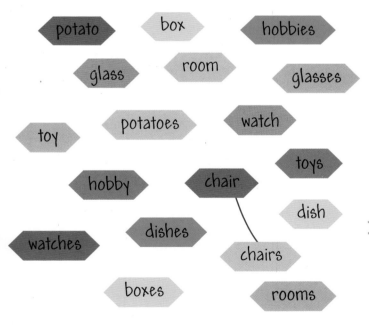

potato   box   hobbies

glass   room   glasses

potatoes   watch

toy   toys

hobby   chair   dish

watches   dishes   chairs

boxes   rooms

8 Write the plurals of these words.

sandwich   class   page   house   address
boy   phone   tomato   match   story

sandwiches

Possessive adjectives – singular

9 Look at the table and label the pictures.

I	you	he	she	it
my	your	his	her	its

1

.... books

2

.... car!

3

.... dad

10 Complete the sentences with the correct possessive adjectives.

1 She's from Spain. _Her_ name is Sara.
2 Tom is fifteen. .... brother is eighteen.
3 I'm French, but .... mum is Moroccan.
4 My sister is ten. .... name is Alexa.
5 This is Ben. Ben is .... friend.
6 This is my horse. .... name is Olli.
7 My best friend's name is George. ....
mum and dad are from the USA.

1B Are they in my class?

Presentation

1 Warm up Match the words with the pictures.

bag [4]   pencil case [ ]   eraser [ ]   keys [ ]   jacket [ ]   money [ ]

1

3

5

2

4

6

2 🔘 **1.32 Read and listen to *Poppy's world* on page 23. Tick (✓) the things you can see from Exercise 1.**

3 🔘 **1.32 Read and listen again. Are the sentences true (*T*) or false (*F*)?**

1 The pencil case is on the table. T
2 The keys are on the table.
3 The mobile phone is in the bag.

4 Jack and Poppy are brother and sister.
5 Jack is thirteen.

4 Read *Language focus*. Then complete the conversations.

1 A Is it your bag, Darius?
  B Yes, it is .
2 A Are you Greek?
  B Yes, I ....
3 A .... your brother at your school?
  B No, he ....
4 A .... your mobile phone in your bag?
  B Yes, it ....

Language focus

- My pencil case **isn't** in my bag!
- **Are** you in my class? **Yes, I am**.
- **Is** my mobile phone on the table? **No, it isn't.**
- **Are** they in my class?
- Jack **isn't** in our class, but Emma **is**.

5 Work in pairs. Ask and answer questions.

A Are you from New York?   B Yes, I am. / No, I'm not.
A Are you twelve?   B Yes, I am. / No, I'm not.
A Is your mobile phone in your bag?   B Yes, it is. / No, it isn't.
A Are your parents Irish?   B Yes, they are. / No, they aren't.
A Is Rihanna your favourite singer? B Yes, she is. / No, she isn't.
A Is your favourite colour red?   B Yes, it is. / No, it isn't.

A **1.32** A new town. A new house. A new school. It's my first day ... and I'm late!

Poppy	Mum, my pencil case isn't in my bag!
Mum	It's on the table, Poppy.
Poppy	Oh no! My keys aren't in my bag!
Mum	They're in your jacket.
Poppy	Is my mobile phone in my jacket?
Mum	No, it isn't. It's here, Poppy.
Poppy	Silly me! Thanks, Mum. See you!

B I'm in the playground with my new friends.

Amy	Hi, I'm Amy.
Poppy	Hi, I'm Poppy. Are you in my class?
Amy	Yes, I am. This is David. He's in your class, too.
Poppy	Hi, David.
David	Hello.
Amy	That's Jack and Emma. They're brother and sister.
Poppy	Are they in our class?
David	Jack isn't in our class, but Emma is.
Poppy	How old is Jack?
David	He's twelve.

C I think Jack is cool!

Jack	Nice mobile.
Poppy	Thanks. Listen to my ringtone. It's great!
Emma	It's the first lesson!
Poppy	And we're late!

Chat zone

I'm late!
Silly me!
See you!
cool

Your space Talking about your friend

6 Complete the sentences about your best friend.

My best friend ¹ _is__ / _isn't_ French.
He / She ² .... twelve.
He / She ³ .... in my class.
His / Her favourite ⁴ .... (*colour*).
His / Her parents ⁵ .... (*nationality*).

be – negative

1 (Circle) the correct words. Use the table to help you.

He *isn't* / *aren't* a good artist!

They *isn't* / *aren't* good tennis players!

negative	short form
I am not	I'm not
you are not	you aren't
he	he isn't
she is not	she isn't
it	it isn't
we	we aren't
you are not	you aren't
they	they aren't

2 Change the sentences to the negative form.

1 I'm English. *I'm not English.*
2 We're in a café. _____
3 They're from Paris. _____
4 Sue's in a hurry. _____
5 He's wrong. _____
6 You're in my class. _____
7 It's an easy exercise. _____

3 ✎ **Work in pairs. Correct the information about you.**

You're in a café.

You're fifteen.

You're in a museum.

You're from England.

No, I'm not in a café. I'm at school.

Soundbite

/aɪ/ /ɪ/

🔊 **1.33 Listen and repeat.**
Hi, I'm Mike. This is Millie.
I'm not Millie. My name's Lizzie.

Hi, I'm Kyla. This is Nick.
I'm not Nick. My name's Rick.

be – questions and short answers

4 **Complete the conversation. Use the table to help you.**

questions		short answers	
Am	I ... ?	Yes, I am.	No, I'm not.
Are	you ... ?	Yes, you are.	No, you aren't.
Is	he ... ?	Yes, he	No, he
	she ... ?	Yes, she is.	No, she isn't.
	it ... ?	Yes, it	No, it
Are	we ... ?	Yes, we	No, we
	you ... ?	Yes, you are.	No, you aren't.
	they ... ?	Yes, they	No, they

Tom: Hello.
Lily: Hi. [1] *Are* you a new student?
Tom: Yes, I [2] _____ .
Lily: [3] _____ you from America?
Tom: No, I [4] _____ . I [5] _____ from Australia.
Lily: Cool! How old [6] _____ you?
Tom: I [7] _____ twelve. [8] _____ you in my class?
Lily: Yes, I [9] _____ .
Tom: [10] _____ they in our class?
Lily: No, they [11] _____ . But Izzy [12] _____ my best friend. And her mum [13] _____ Australian, too!

5 🔊 **1.34 Listen and check. Then act out the conversation with a partner.**

6 ✏️ **Write the questions.**

1 in your class / your best friend / is ?
   Is your best friend in your class?
2 at home / your parents / are ?
3 is / old / your computer ?
4 your favourite actor / Zac Efron / is ?
5 is / very big / your school ?
6 a good singer / you / are ?

7 ✏️ **Answer the questions for you.**

Is your best friend in your class?
Yes, she is.

8 ✏️ **Complete the form for your partner. Don't ask questions!**

Name	
Age	
Nationality	
Favourite colour	
Favourite book	
Favourite TV programme	

9 💬 **Work in pairs. Ask questions to check your ideas.**

A Are you eleven?
B Yes, I am.

Articles

10 **Look at the boxes. Write a, an or the.**

a + consonant	*an* + vowel
a banana a guitar	an apple an umbrella

the + all letters
the sun the moon

1 a. computer 2 ...... bicycle
3 ...... bag 4 ...... eraser 5 ...... Earth
6 ...... pen 7 ...... exercise book
8 ...... cat 9 ...... orange 10 ...... football

→ **Language check page 138**

be

Age

*How old **are** you?*
I'm twelve.

Nationality and place

*Where **are** you from?*
I'm from Mars.

Descriptions

*Our classroom **is** small.*

Favourites

*My favourite colour **is** green.*

Jobs

*My mum **is** an artist.*

11 ✏️ **Complete the sentences about you. Use the verb be.**

1 I .... (*nationality*)
2 I .... (*age*)
3 My best friend .... (*age*)
4 My favourite actor .... (*name*)
5 My mobile phone .... (*colour*)
6 My classroom .... (*description*)

12 **Read your sentences to your partner.**

1C Skills

Reading

1 Warm up Read the webpage quickly and answer the questions.

How old are the students? Are they boys or girls?

2 Read the webpage again and write the names of the people.

1 He's from Sweden. *Pet King*
2 Her favourite superhero is Batman.
3 She's from America.
4 They're thirteen.

5 He's twelve.
6 Tubby is his hamster.
7 She's from Manchester.
8 They're football fans.

Penpal SPACE

home **my posting** **club members** **class** **penpal** **help**

Hello. I'm thirteen. I'm from Chicago, USA. My pets are a crazy dog and three fish. My hobbies are computer games and swimming. I'm a girl. Are you a girl or boy? Please write.
Snowgirl

Snowgirl

Hi there! I'm from Manchester in England and I'm twelve. I'm a girl and I'm in a basketball team. It's my favourite sport. My favourite superhero is Batman. I think he's cool. Are you a girl? Are you twelve or thirteen? Then please be my penpal!!!

Batgirl

Hello. I'm a Swedish boy and I'm thirteen. My interests are tennis, music and computer games. I'm a Liverpool fan. It's my favourite football team. My favourite films are *Lord of the Rings* and *Spider-Man*. My pets are Fluffy (a cat), Zed (a dog) and Tubby (a hamster). Write to me, please!

Pet King

Hi! I'm from Beijing, China. I'm a boy and I'm twelve. My favourite sports are basketball and football. My favourite things are my England football shirt, my computer and my DVDs. Please be my penpal!

Dylan Dog

Vocabulary • Interests

3 🔊 **1.36 Match the words with the pictures. Then listen and check.**

science 3   sport ☐   animals ☐   books ☐   art ☐
computer games ☐   films ☐   fashion ☐   the internet ☐   music ☐

1
2
3
4
5

6
7
8
9
10

Listening and speaking

4 🔊 **1.37 Listen and circle the correct answer.**

	Lucy	Kasun
Age	12 (13)	11 12
Birthday	March May	June July
From	England Ireland	France Greece
Interests	science animals music	art computers sport
Favourite singer	Beyoncé Alicia Keys	Justin Bieber Will.i.am
Favourite thing	mobile phone dog	football shirt computer

Lucy

Kasun

5 **Work in pairs. Ask and answer questions.**
A How old are you?   **B** I'm twelve.

6 **Tell the class about your partner. Use the model to help you.**
Martia is twelve. Her birthday is in April. She's from Spain. Her interests are films and fashion. Her favourite singer is Madonna. Her favourite thing is her computer.

Writing

7 **Write your profile for the Penpal Space webpage.**
Hello. I'm a ¹............. (*boy / girl*) and I'm ²............. (*age*)
I'm from ³............. . (*country*)
My interests are ⁴............. , ⁵............. and ⁶............. .
My favourite film/singer/football team is ⁷............. .
Please be my penpal.
(*Invent an English name!*)

Study skills

In English, write countries and nationalities with a capital letter.
England – English

➡ **Communication page 118**   ➡ **Your Space Web Zone**

Grammar
be – question words •
there is, there are • lots of •
irregular plurals

Functions
talking about homes

Vocabulary • The house

1 ⊙ **1.40** **Match the words with the rooms in the house. Then listen and check.**
bathroom [10]   kitchen [ ]   study [ ]   living room [ ]   hall [ ]
bedroom [ ]   garden [ ]   dining room [ ]   toilet [ ]   garage [ ]

Presentation

2 **Warm up** **Look at *Poppy's world* on page 29. Answer the questions.**
What are the rooms? Who are the people in the photos?

3 ⊙ **1.41** **Listen and read the photo story. Are the sentences true (*T*) or false (*F*)?**

1 There are two bedrooms in the house. F
2 There's one bathroom.
3 Poppy isn't late.

4 There's a small living room.
5 Poppy and Josh aren't late for school.
6 It's Friday morning.

4 ⊙ **1.42** **Read *Language focus*. Complete the descriptions with *there's* or *there are*. Then listen and check.**

Amy In my house, ¹..there...are... only two bedrooms. There isn't a dining room, but
²_____ a big kitchen. ³_____ a big garden, too. It's a fantastic house.

Jack ⁴_____ three bedrooms in my house. ⁵_____ one for me, one for Emma, and
one for our parents. ⁶_____ a small kitchen, but ⁷_____ a big living room.
It's my favourite room.

5 **Work in pairs. Say true and false things about your house. Is your partner telling the truth or not?**
Use these words:
There's _____ . There are _____ . There isn't _____ .

6 **Describe your house to your partner.**
There's a big garden. There isn't a dining room.

Language focus

• **There's** only one bathroom.
• **There are** three bedrooms.
• **Where are** my trainers?
• **What's** the time?

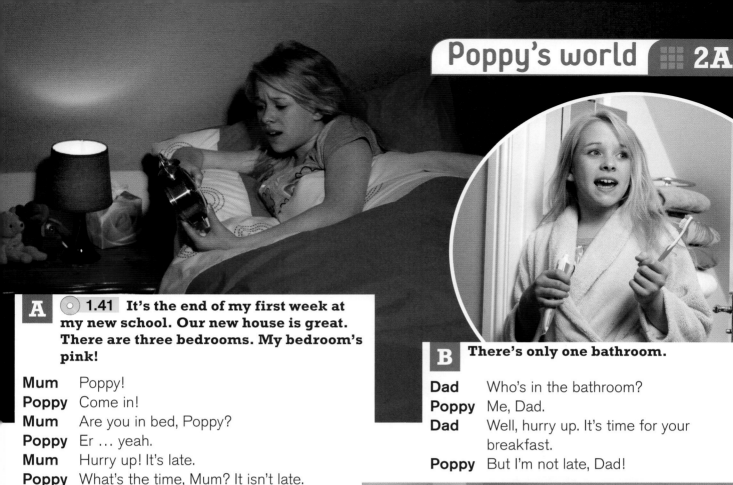

A ◉ 1.41 **It's the end of my first week at my new school. Our new house is great. There are three bedrooms. My bedroom's pink!**

Mum	Poppy!
Poppy	Come in!
Mum	Are you in bed, Poppy?
Poppy	Er … yeah.
Mum	Hurry up! It's late.
Poppy	What's the time, Mum? It isn't late. It's early!

B **There's only one bathroom.**

Dad	Who's in the bathroom?
Poppy	Me, Dad.
Dad	Well, hurry up. It's time for your breakfast.
Poppy	But I'm not late, Dad!

C **There's a big kitchen. It's busy in the morning.**

Poppy	Where are the cornflakes? They aren't here.
Josh	I don't know. Where are my trainers?
Poppy	Ha ha ha!
Josh	What's so funny?
Poppy	They're on your feet, silly!

D **There's a big living room, too. It's cool!**

Mum	You're late for school.
Poppy	No, we aren't, Mum.
Mum	But it's half past eight!
Poppy	It's Saturday, Mum. There's no school today!

My parents are great. But they're strange, too!

Your space   Talking about your life

7 **Work in pairs. Ask and answer the questions.**
How old are you? Where are you from? Who are your favourite singers / bands? What's your favourite film? When is your birthday?

8 **Write sentences about your partner.**
Michelle is eleven. She's from Paris. Her favourite singer is Shakira …

Chat zone
Come in!
Hurry up!
I don't know.
What's so funny?

Question words and *be*

1 **Complete the cartoon. Use the table to help you.**

.... is your cat?

He's twenty. He's very old.

.... is he now?

He's at home.

Question words
Where are you from?
Who's your class teacher?
What's your name?
When's your birthday?
What's your favourite colour?
How old are you?
How are you?

Get it right!

Remember to use the correct form of the verb:

My chairs are very comfortable.

NOT ~~My chairs is very comfortable.~~

Where are you from?

NOT ~~Where is you from?~~

2 ☆ **Work in pairs. Ask your partner the questions in the table.**

A Where are you from?
B I'm from Turkey.

3 **Complete the questions with the question words.**

1 ..Where.... is Kylie Minogue from?
2 .... is that girl in the photo?
3 .... is your favourite food?
4 .... are my school books?
5 .... is your sister?
6 .... is your English lesson?
7 How .... you?

4 **Match the answers to the questions in Exercise 3.**

She's my friend.

She's from Australia.   It's ice cream.

They're in your bag!   She's seventeen.

It's this morning.   I'm twelve.

5 ⊙ **1.43** **Listen and complete the table.**

PENFRIENDS AROUND THE WORLD	Luis	Jade
Name	Luis	Jade
Age	12	
Birthday		
From	Mexico	
Favourite colour		orange
Favourite food		

6 ☆ **Work in pairs. Cover the table. Ask and answer questions.**

A How old is Luis?   B He's twelve.

7 **Invent a new character. Copy and complete the table.**

Name	Super Alex

8 ☆ **Work in pairs. Ask and answer questions with your partner.**

A What's your name?   B Super Alex!

there is / there are

positive	negative	questions	short answers
there is	there isn't	Is there ...?	Yes, there is. / No, there isn't.
there are	there aren't	Are there ...?	Yes, there are. / No, there aren't.

9 Complete the sentences with **there is** or **there are**. Use the table to help you.

1 *There is a* photo on the wall.
2 .... computer on the desk.
3 .... girl in the room.
4 .... two windows.
5 .... two doors.
6 .... TV on the desk.
7 .... two beds in the room.
8 .... guitar on the bed.

10 ☆ **Work in pairs. Close your book. Ask your partner about the picture.**

A Is there a ... ?   B Yes, there is. / No, there isn't.

A Are there ... ?   B Yes, there are. / No, there aren't.

lots of

11 **Complete the sentences with a, *an* and *lots of*.**

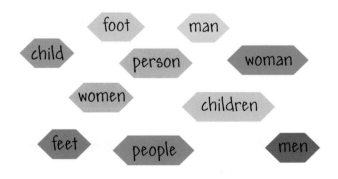
Welcome to my school!

1 There are lots of windows in my classroom.
2 There is .... map in my classroom.
3 There is .... orange in my school bag.
4 There is .... library in our school.
5 There are .... computers in our library.
6 There are .... teachers in the teachers' room.
7 There is .... tree in our playground.
8 There are .... cars at the school at 3.00.

12 ✎ **Write a description of the classroom.**

In my classroom there are three windows and one door ...

Irregular plurals

13 **Match the singulars and the plurals.**

foot   man
child   person   woman
women   children
feet   people   men

14 **Write the plurals of these words. Some are regular.**

1 desk   2 child   3 bus   4 boy
5 class   6 man   7 door   8 story
9 day   10 watch   11 foot   12 hobby

15 ◉ **1.44**   **Listen and check.**

Grammar

this, that, these, those •
possessive adjectives •
prepostions of place

Functions
describing rooms

Vocabulary • Bedroom

1 ◯ **1.45 Warm up** Look at Liam's room on page 33 and write the numbers next to the words. Then listen and check.

TV [5]　　 desk ☐　 bed ☐　 armchair ☐　 bookcase ☐
wardrobe ☐　 lamp ☐　 rug ☐　 posters ☐　 cushions ☐

2 **Work in pairs. Talk about Liam's room.**
There's a desk. There are lots of books.

Presentation

3 ◯ **1.46** Read and listen to Liam's webpage.
Then answer the questions.

　 1 Who is on the posters? His favourite footballers.
　 2 What is on his desk?
　 3 Where are his cushions from? And his rug?
　 4 What is on his walls?
　 5 Where are his school books?
　 6 What is his favourite thing?

4 Read *Language focus*. Then (circle) *this, that,*
these and *those* on Liam's webpage.

5 **Choose room A or room B. Imagine that this is your bedroom and you are the person in the room. Describe the room to your partner.**
This is my desk. Those are my CDs.

Language focus

- **This** is an old armchair.
- **These** are my favourite books.
- **That's** my wardrobe.
- **Those** are my school books.

A

B

1.46

My room 'A mess? It's perfect!'
says Liam Murray

That's my wardrobe. It's next to the window. Don't look in it – it's a mess!

Those posters on the wall are of my favourite footballers.

There's lots of stuff on my desk! That's my new computer. And behind the computer there's an old lamp.

That is my TV. It's next to the desk.

There are lots of books in my bookcase.

Those are my school books under the bed. Oh dear!

This is my favourite thing. It's my new guitar!

This rug is from the market. It's cool.

This is an old armchair for my friends. These cushions are from our holiday in Morocco.

These are my favourite books. They're brilliant!

Your space   Describing my room

6 **Draw your bedroom. Then write sentences about it.**

This is my desk.
There's a TV next to the wardrobe.
These are my posters.

7 **Work in pairs. Tell your partner about your bedroom.**

There are two beds.

Chat zone
stuff
It's a mess!
Oh dear!

this, that, these, those

1   Complete the sentences with *this / that / these / those*.

1 .... cats
are very naughty!

2 .... is my
old house.

3 ....armchair
is very old.

4 .... mobile
phones are very small.

5 .... cars
are amazing!

6 .... is
my lunch!

7 .... present
is for you.

8 .... mobile
phones are
expensive.

Prepositions of place

2   Match the prepositions with the pictures.

behind ☐   in ☐   in front of ☐   near 1   next to ☐   opposite ☐   on ☐   under ☐

3   ✎ Write sentences about the room.

1 the football / the school bag
  The football is behind the school bag.
2 the computer / the desk
3 the mobile phone / the apple
4 the books / the bed
5 the ruler / the bag
6 the trainers / the wardrobe
7 the cat / the curtains

Soundbite

/s/ /z/ /ɪz/

🔊 1.47   Listen and repeat.

1 /s/	2 /z/	3 /ɪz/
desks	names	pages
months	days	houses
shirts	birds	classes
books	windows	boxes
lakes	posters	glasses

Possessive adjectives

4 ⊙ **1.48** **Complete the sentences. Use the table to help you. Listen and check.**

subject	possessive adjective
I	my
you	your
he	his
she	her
it	its
we	our
you	your
they	their

1 Chloe and _her_ brother go to my school.
2 Hi, I'm Sophie. .... favourite singer is Rihanna.
3 My dog is black and white. .... name is Spot.
4 We love football. .... favourite team is Leeds United.
5 My friends are on holiday with .... parents.
6 My Art teacher is Mr Smith. .... lessons are really interesting.

5 ⊙ **1.49** **Complete the penpal site. Listen and check.**

○○○ **new message**

Hi

¹............... name's Ellie. I'm twelve.
My brother is Dan. He's eighteen and
²............... favourite sport is football.
My sister is nine. ³............... name is
Ros. We are from London and ⁴...............
house is near the Arsenal football
stadium. My mum and dad are doctors
and ⁵............... lives are very busy.
Write to me soon. Tell me about you
and ⁶............... life!

Ellie

6 ✏ **Write to Ellie about you.**

⟩ **Language check page 138**

adjectives

7 **Find the opposites. Copy and complete the table.**

Adjectives	
funny	serious

funny

small

new

early

horrible

big

late

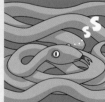
long

old

short

nice

serious

8 ✏ **Complete the sentences about you. Use an adjective.**

1 My mobile phone is ....
2 My house is ....
3 I've got a new ....
4 I've got an old ....
5 .... is funny.
6 .... is horrible.

Reading

1 Warm up Match the headings with the pictures.

A home in a cave ☐   A home in a forest ☐   A home in a boat ☐

Home sweet home

1

Three teenagers tell us about their amazing homes.

This is my home on a river in England. What is it? It's a houseboat! It is very small but there is a kitchen, a living room and two bedrooms. There is a TV and a computer, too. It's great!

2

My family's wooden house is in the countryside in Poland. It's in a forest and near a lake. There are lots of animals and birds. We are very happy here.

3

This is my holiday home. It's a cave in Spain! There's a living room, three bedrooms, a bathroom and a kitchen. I love this house – it's very cosy, and it's fun, too. In the town there are cave cinemas, cave restaurants and cave cafés!

2 Read about the houses and answer the questions. Write *cave*, *boat* or *forest*.

Which home …

1 is very quiet? *cave* **4** is very small?

2 is on a river? **5** is near cinemas and restaurants?

3 is near a lake? **6** is near animals and birds?

Listening and speaking

3 ◉ **1.51** Listen to Natasha and Sanjit and complete the table.

	house or apartment	number of bedrooms	other rooms
Natasha	....	....	kitchen ....
Sanjit	....	....	....

> **Study skills**
>
> **Vocabulary notebook**
> • Make a *Vocabulary notebook*. Write the new words you find in each unit. Divide the words into subject groups.
> **Rooms:** bedroom, bathroom …
> **Things in a bedroom:** bed, wardrobe …
> **Places:** lake, forest …

4 ◉ **1.51** Listen again. Which is Sanjit's favourite room? Why?

5 Work in pairs. Describe your house to your partner. Say which is your favourite room and why.

In my house there are two bedrooms. There is a nice living room and a small kitchen. My favourite room is my bedroom!

Speaking and writing

6 Imagine your dream house.
- Is it in a city / by the sea / in the countryside?
- Is it a house / an apartment / a castle?
- Is there a music room / a games room / a gym, etc.?
- Is there a swimming pool / a tennis court / a cinema, etc.?

7 Work in pairs. Describe your dream house to your partner.

My dream house is in London. It is a big palace. There are 100 rooms. There are 20 bedrooms. My favourite room is the cinema.

8 Write about your dream house.

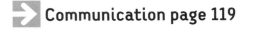 

Vocabulary • Family

1 **2.02** **Complete the table with the words. Then listen and check.**

aunt   brother   wife   cousin   grandfather   father

♀	♂	♂♀
mother		parents
stepmother	stepfather	
	husband	X
sister		X
	uncle	X
grandmother		grandparents
daughter	son	children
cousin		cousins

2 **Look at Dylan's family tree on page 39 and write the missing family words.**

Presentation

3 Warm up **Look at the photo of Dylan on page 39 and answer the questions.**

How old is he? Where is he from?

4 **2.03** **Read and listen to the interview about Dylan's family. Are the sentences true (*T*) or false (*F*)?**

1 Dylan's got a brother and a sister. T
2 He's got one aunt.
3 His father has got two sisters.
4 His mother has got one brother.
5 He's got three cousins.
6 He's got four grandparents.

Language focus

- Chloe's new boyfriend is very nice.
- My mum's parents are British.
- Auntie Sarah and Uncle Tim's children are Nick and Jessica.
- **I've got** a brother and a sister.
- My **dad's got** a sister.
- **They've got** a house with a swimming pool.

5 **Read *Language focus* and look at Dylan's family tree. Then complete the sentences.**

1 Pete is John's *father* .
2 Nick is Dylan's _____ .
3 Pete is Tom and Oliver's _____ .
4 Kevin is _____ and _____ father.
5 Jessica is _____ and _____ daughter.
6 Tom is _____ brother.

6 **Work in pairs. Say true and false sentences about Dylan.**

A Jenny is Pete's wife.   **B** True.
A Tim is Clare's brother.   **B** False.

Pete Adams *grandfather* + Jenny Adams

Kevin Marsh + Helen Marsh *grandmother*

Jo *aunt* + John *uncle*

Clare *mother* + Rob *father*

Sarah *aunt* + Tim *uncle*

Tom *cousin*   Oliver *cousin*   Chloe *sister*   Dylan   Ben   Nick   Jessica

meet the family

2.03

This is an interview with my epal, Dylan in Sydney, Australia. Dylan is my age. He's twelve. He's got an interesting family.

Tell me about your family, Dylan. Is it big?
No, it isn't. It's small! My mum's name is Clare and my dad's name is Rob. And I've got a brother and a sister. Chloe is sixteen and Ben's ten. Chloe's new boyfriend is very nice. His name is Dylan, too!
I've only got four uncles and aunts. My dad's got a sister (my Auntie Sarah). Her husband is Uncle Tim. My mum's got a brother (my Uncle John). He's from London. Uncle John's wife is my Auntie Jo.

What about cousins?
I've got four cousins! My British cousins are Tom and Oliver. Tom is twelve and Oliver is only three. Auntie Sarah and Uncle Tim's children are Nick and Jessica. Nick has got a job in New York.

Tell me about your grandparents.
Gran and Grandad Marsh are my dad's parents. They've got a house with a swimming pool near our house! My mum's parents, Gran and Grandad Adams, are British.

That's fantastic! Thanks for the interview, Dylan.
That's OK. Interviews are fun!

Your space   Talking about families

7   **Work in pairs. Describe your family to your partner.**
I've got a small family. My mum's name is Leah. My dad's name is Sam. I've got one sister. Her name is Julia. I've got two uncles and two aunts. And I've got three cousins.

have got – positive

1 Complete the cartoon with short forms of *have got*. Use the tables to help you.

full form		short form	
I	have got	I've	got
you		you've	
he	has got	he's	got
she		she's	
it		it's	
we	have got	we've	got
you		you've	
they		they've	

I _____ lots of friends on Roboweb.

And you _____ lots of toys!

Lara _____ ten cousins.

2 📖 Read and complete the email. Use the short forms of *have got* where possible.

Hi

My name's Antony. I'm 13. I ¹ _ve got a sister, Cath, and a brother, Matt. We ² _____ a big dog. Its name is Fido. Cath's hobby is music. She ³ _____ a really good stereo. Matt ⁴ _____ lots of DVDs in his room – his hobby is cinema. I ⁵ _____ a friend in New Zealand, Mark. He ⁶ _____ a big family. They ⁷ _____ a big house in the mountains. It ⁸ _____ ten bedrooms! Our house in England ⁹ _____ three bedrooms, but we ¹⁰ _____ a big garden.

Write soon!

A ☺

3 ⊙ **2.04** What have the teenagers got? Listen and tick (✓).

	Katie	Tom	Ella	Ahmed
computer	✓			
mp3 player	✓			
camera				
guitar				
bicycle				

 Get it right!

Remember to use the possessive *'s*:

She is my mother's cousin.

NOT ~~She is the cousin of my mother.~~

4 Complete the sentences with the short form of *have got*.

1 Katie _'s got_ a computer and an mp3 player.
2 Tom and Ahmed _____ a guitar.
3 Ella _____ a computer, an _____ and a _____ .
4 Katie and Ella _____ an mp3 player.
5 Ella _____ a bicycle.
6 Tom and Ahmed _____ a camera.

5 Complete the table for you.

	you	
computer		
mp3 player		
camera		
guitar		
bicycle		

6 Work in pairs. Tell your partner your information. Listen and complete the table for your partner.

7 Write sentences about you and your partner.

I've got a / an … .
Anna's got a / an … .

Possessive 's

8 Match the sentences with the pictures.

a They're Paul and Rosie's dogs.   4
b It's Laura and Mike's dog.
c It's Harry's dog.
d They're Luke's dogs.

1  2
3  4

9 Write sentences. Use the possessive *'s*.

1 His schoolbag is new. (Steve)
  Steve's schoolbag is new.
2 His English teacher is Mr Day. (Radimir)
3 Their computer is new. (Stef and Cara)
4 Her bike is in the playground. (Pam)
5 Their house is in this road. (Jo and Tom)
6 Her car is in the car park. (Mrs Morgan)

10 ⊙ **2.05** Listen and match the people with the things.

a Alisha   b Will   c Uncle Cam
d Reem   e Mrs Brooke
f Alex and Kate   g Owen   h Kylie

1

2

3

4

5

6

7

8

11 Work in pairs. Talk about the people and things.

A Whose car is this?
B It's Mrs Brooke's.

3B I haven't got my mobile!

Grammar
have got – negative form •
have got – questions and
short answers • *Whose ...?*
and possessive pronouns

Functions
talking about possessions

Vocabulary • People

1 (○) **2.06 Match the words with the pictures. Then listen and check.**

friendly [6]   shy [ ]   funny [ ]   kind [ ]   serious [ ]   clever [ ]

1	2	3

4	5	6

2 **Work in pairs. Talk about people you know.**

Lisa is friendly. My brother is shy.

Presentation

3 **Warm up Look at *Poppy's world* on page 43 and answer the questions.**
Who are the people in the photos? Where are they?

4 (○) **2.07 Listen and read the photo story. Then complete the sentences with
the names.**

1 _David_ is shy.
2 .... is friendly and kind.
3 .... is serious.
4 .... is clever.
5 .... is Poppy's best friend.
6 .... is funny.

Language focus

- **Have you got** your homework?
- Yes, **we have**. / No, **I haven't**.
- I **haven't got** my mobile.
- He **hasn't got** a good memory.

5 **Read the photo story again. Whose are these things?**
1 the science magazine ....
2 the hat ....
3 the mobile phone ....

6 **Read *Language focus*. Find the sentences in the photo story. Can you find two
more sentences with *have got*?**

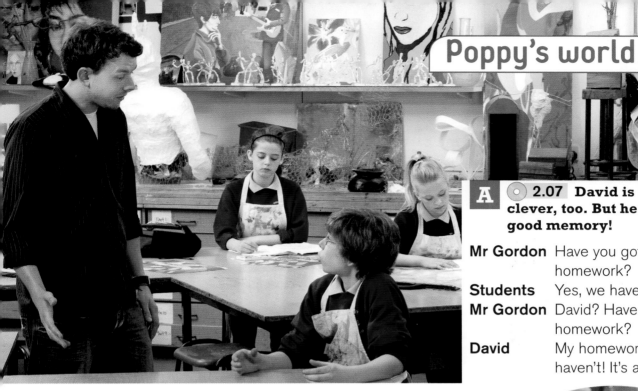

A 🔘 2.07 **David is shy. He's clever, too. But he hasn't got a good memory!**

Mr Gordon	Have you got your homework?
Students	Yes, we have.
Mr Gordon	David? Have you got your homework?
David	My homework? No, I haven't! It's at home!

B **Jack and Emma are brother and sister. They're very different. Emma is serious but Jack's funny. And they haven't got the same interests.**

Jack	Whose is this science magazine?
Emma	It's mine. It's interesting.
Jack	You're joking!
Emma	Is this hat yours?
Jack	Yes, it is.
Emma	Well, I think it's silly!

C **Have you got a best friend? I have! Her name's Amy. She's my age. She's friendly and kind.**

Poppy	Oh no! I haven't got my mobile!
Amy	Where is it?
Poppy	It's in my other bag!
Amy	Don't worry. Here's mine.
Poppy	Oh thanks, Amy. You're a star!

Your space · Talking about possessions

7 **Work in pairs and ask and answer questions. Use these words.**

horse   swimming pool   dog   skateboard   DVD player   cat

A Have you got a bicycle?   **B** Yes, I have.
                               C No, I haven't.

8 **Tell the class about your partner.**
Sofia hasn't got a horse, but she's got a cat.

Chat zone
You're joking!
Don't worry.
You're a star!

have got – negative

1 Match the sentences with the cartoons. Use the table to help you.

a We haven't got our books.

b It hasn't got a camera.

c I haven't got an umbrella.

d She hasn't got a key.

full form			short form		
I you	have not		I you	haven't	
he she it	has not	got	he she it	hasn't	got
we you they	have not		we you they	haven't	

2 ⊙ **2.08** Listen and tick (✓) or cross (✗).

	Finlay	Emma	Nick and Suzy
lizard	✔		
spider	✗		
snake			
parrot			
tortoise			
frog			

3 ✎ Write sentences about the friends.

Finlay has got a lizard but …

4 ☆ Work in pairs. Talk about you and your family's pets.

A I've got a cat.
B My uncle's got two horses!

have got – questions and short answers

questions			short answers					
Have	I you		Yes,	I you	have.	No,	I you	haven't.
Has	he she it	got …?	Yes,	he she it	has.	No,	he she it	hasn't.
Have	we you they		Yes,	we you they	have.	No,	we you they	haven't.

5 ⊙ **2.09** Complete the conversations. Then listen and check.

1 Adam: _Have_ you _got_ a pencil?
Tyler: Yes, I _____ .
Adam: And an eraser and a ruler?
Tyler: Adam, _____ you _____ your bag?
Adam: No, I _____ .

2 Jack: _____ Lucy _____ her dictionary?
Esme: Yes, she _____ .

3 Maria: _____ your parents _____ a new computer?
Paige: Yes, they _____ .

4 Teacher: Zoe, Faith. _____ you _____ your homework?
Zoe and Faith: No, we _____ . Sorry.

6 ✏️ **Put the words in the correct order. Write questions and short answers.**

1 they / a new teacher / have / got / ? (✓)
Have they got a new teacher?
Yes, they have.
2 Ella / a pet dog / have / Mia / got / and / ? (✓)
3 mum / a new job / has / got / your / ? (✓)
4 they / have / lots of cousins / got / ? (✗)
5 she / has / lots of homework / got / ? (✓)
6 a digital camera / you / got / have / ? (✗)

7 🗨️ **Work in pairs. Write the names of three people you know. Ask your partner questions about them.**

A Has your friend Sarah got a car?
B Yes, she has.

Possessive pronouns and Whose ... ?

subject	possessive adjective	possessive pronoun
I	my	mine
you	your	yours
he	his	his
she	her	hers
it	its	–
we	our	ours
you	your	yours
they	their	theirs

8 **Complete the sentences.**

1 It's your DVD. It's _yours_ .
2 This isn't my money. It isn't _____ .
3 They're Matt's parents. They're _____ .
4 Is this bag Sophie's? Is it _____ ?
5 _____ books are these? Are they Li's?
6 It's Kim and Anna's computer game. It's _____ .
7 Are these your keys? Are they _____ ?
8 It's my brother's new mp3. It's _____ .
9 _____ bag is this? Is it yours?
10 They're our posters. They're _____ .

➡️ **Language check page 139**

  's

9 **Match the pictures with the sentences.**

be • Use *'s* in place of *is*.

  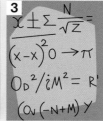

He**'s** ninety-nine. [2]
It**'s** difficult. ☐
She**'s** a doctor. ☐

have got • Use *'s* in place of *has*.

She**'s got** lots of books. ☐
He**'s got** a new computer. ☐
It**'s got** a free CD. ☐

's • Use *'s* with possessions.

Jake and Dan**'s** house is very small. ☐
Is this your mum**'s** car? ☐
This is Ruby**'s** mobile phone. ☐

10 **Read the sentences. Write *be*, *have got* or *'s*.**

1 He's got an old car. _have got_
2 Jenni's mobile phone is red. _____
3 It's Monday today. _____
4 It's got small windows. _____
5 Is he your sister's friend? _____
6 She's from Poland. _____

Vocabulary • Describing people

1 🔘 2.11 **Label the pictures with the words. Then listen and check.**

| blue   fair   straight   slim   green   short |

Build

1 tall   **2** ....   **3** plump   **4** short

Eye colour

5 brown **6** grey   **7** ....   **8** ....

Hair type

9 long   **10** ....   **11** curly   **12** ....

Hair colour

13 dark   **14** ....

Reading and writing

2 **Look at the film poster and answer the questions.**

1 What is the title of the film?   **3** What is their address?
2 Who are *The Fantastic Five*?   **4** When is the film on at the cinema?

There's a new family of Superheroes. They've got super powers.
And they've got a little house at 55 Orbit Road, Brighton. Who are they?

THE FANTASTIC FIVE

See their new adventure...

In cinemas on 1st July!

3 **Match the descriptions with the Fantastic Five. Write the numbers.**

[5] Amber is tall and slim. She's got long red hair and brown eyes. She's thirty-eight.

[ ] George is fifteen. He's got short straight hair and he's got glasses. He's short and plump.

[ ] Elliot is short and plump. He's got short straight hair. He hasn't got glasses. He's only five.

[ ] Holly is sixteen. She is short and slim. She's got green eyes and curly red hair.

[ ] Roger is very tall and slim. He's got long dark hair and brown eyes. He's forty.

4 **Draw your own superhero and write a description.**

Listening and speaking

5 ◉ **2.12** **Listen to Lauren and write the names and the family words.**

Ben   Sue   Lauren   Ellie   ~~Katie~~   David

1 Katie
She's Lauren's mum.

2

3

4

5

6

6 ◉ **2.12** **Draw lines from the names to the pictures. Listen again and check.**

7 **Work in pairs. Describe your family.**
My brother is eleven. He's tall and he's got short dark hair. He's funny.

Grammar
present simple – positive
form • prepositions of time

Functions
saying when you do things

Presentation

1 **Warm up** Look at the pictures on page 49 and find:

a football   dinner   a clock   a computer   breakfast   homework

2 Read Liam's webpage and number the pictures in the correct order.

3 ⊙ **2.17**   Read the sentences about Liam. Are they true (*T*) or false (*F*)?
Then listen and check.

1 Liam is twelve years old. *T*
2 He lives in Oxford.
3 He has toast and jam and tea for breakfast.
4 He goes to school with his mum.

5 School starts at 8:15 am.
6 His favourite meal is fish and chips.
7 He has football practice on Tuesday.
8 He goes to bed at 11 pm.

Vocabulary • Daily routine

4 ⊙ **2.18**   Match the words with the pictures. Then listen and check.

get dressed ☐   have dinner ☐   have breakfast ☐   watch TV ☐   go to bed ☐
get up 1   have lunch ☐   do homework 7   get washed ☐   go to school ☐

5 ⊙ **2.19**   Read *Language focus*. Then listen and write
the times in Molly's day.

Molly's day
Molly gets up at ¹ quarter past seven . She has breakfast
at ² _____ . She goes to school at ³ _____ .
School starts at ⁴ _____ and finishes at ⁵ _____ .
Molly gets home at ⁶ _____ . The family has dinner at
⁷ _____ . Then they watch TV. Molly goes to bed at
⁸ _____ .

Language focus

- I **read** a book before I
  go to sleep at about ten
  o'clock at night.
- Dad **gets** home at
  about six o'clock **in the
  evening**.
- School **starts** at quarter
  to nine.

My project   ◉ 2.17

A day in the life of Liam

My name is Liam and I'm twelve. I live in Cambridge in the UK. On school days I get up at seven o'clock in the morning. I get washed and I get dressed. Then I have breakfast – jam on toast and a glass of orange juice.

I go to school with my friends at quarter past eight. School starts at quarter to nine and finishes at quarter past three. I have lunch at school.

After school I do my homework and chat with my friends on the computer. Dad gets home at about six o'clock in the evening. We have dinner at about half past six. My favourite meal is pasta. I like pizza, too!

On Tuesday I go to football practice. In the evening we watch TV. I go to bed at about half past nine. I read a book before I go to sleep at about ten o'clock at night.

A

B

C

D

E

F

G

Your space   Talking about your routine

6   Work with a partner. Talk about your daily routine.

A I get up at seven o'clock.   B I get up at quarter past six!

Present simple – positive

1 Read the conversation and (circle) the correct form of the verbs. Use the table to help you.

Present simple	
I / you / we / they	eat
he / she / it	eat**s**

Lara What's wrong, Zak?

Zak Well, I ¹ *wake up / wakes up* at eight o'clock and I ² *take / takes* Robopet for a walk. Then I ³ *make / makes* lunch. In the afternoon we ⁴ *go / goes* to the park. And in the evening I ⁵ *watch / watches* TV and Robopet ⁶ *play / plays* videogames. It's boring!

2 Complete the sentences with the present simple. Use the spelling rules below to help you.

Present simple spelling rules		
go	→	go**es**
wash	→	wash**es**
watch	→	watch**es**
have	→	ha**s**
study	→	stud**ies**
play	→	play**s**

1 Luke _goes_ (go) to the cinema every week.

2 Hassan _____ (play) football in the school team.

3 Jane _____ (do) her homework before dinner.

4 My brother _____ (study) French at school.

5 Mohsin _____ (watch) TV after dinner.

6 My mum _____ (finish) work at 7:30 pm.

7 My dad _____ (buy) books on the internet.

8 My sister is one year old. She _____ (cry) a lot.

3 📖 Read and complete the email. Use the present simple.

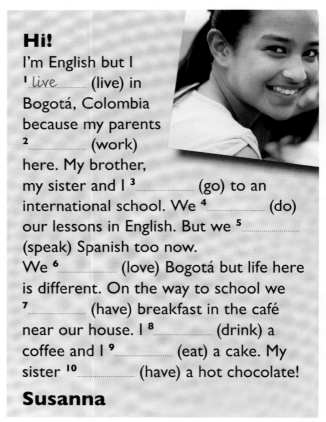

Hi!

I'm English but I ¹ _live_ (live) in Bogotá, Colombia because my parents ² _____ (work) here. My brother, my sister and I ³ _____ (go) to an international school. We ⁴ _____ (do) our lessons in English. But we ⁵ _____ (speak) Spanish too now. We ⁶ _____ (love) Bogotá but life here is different. On the way to school we ⁷ _____ (have) breakfast in the café near our house. I ⁸ _____ (drink) a coffee and I ⁹ _____ (eat) a cake. My sister ¹⁰ _____ (have) a hot chocolate!

Susanna

4 ✏ Write an email to Susanna. Describe your daily routine.

Get it right!

Remember the third person *s*:
She likes football.
NOT ~~She like football.~~

Prepositions of time

5 **Match the expressions with the pictures.**

in	the morning
	the afternoon
	the evening
at	night

1

2

3

4

Soundbite

(**Sentence stress**)

◉ **2.20** **Listen and repeat.**

He **gets up** at **night**
At **half past one,**
Then he **runs out** the **door**
And he **has** some **fun.**

He **gets home** in the **morning**
And he **sits** on the **mat,**
Then he **sleeps** all **day,**
He's a **really lazy cat!**

---

6 🖉 **Write six sentences about the life of a famous person.**

She gets up at 11 o'clock in the morning.

7 🗨 **Work in pairs. Tell your sentences to your partner. Don't say the name! Guess the famous person.**

A She gets up at ten o'clock in the morning. She sings and dances. She's got dark hair and dark skin.
B Beyoncé!

8 🗨 **Tell your partner when you do these things.**

I get up at seven o'clock.

(get up) (go to school) (have lunch)

(come home) (do your homework)

(have dinner) (watch TV) (go to bed)

9 🖉 **Write two true sentences and one false sentence about you. Use these verbs.**

listen to, have, drink, like, play, live, read, study, go, love, eat, get up, wake up, do, watch

10 🗨 **Work in pairs. Tell your partner your sentences. Which sentence is false?**

Grammar
present simple – negative form • present simple – questions and short answers

Functions
talking about free time and hobbies

Vocabulary • Free time activities

1 ⊙ **2.21** **Listen and tick (✓) three activities you like.**

play football ☐   play computer games ☐   write poems and stories ☐
meet friends ☐   read books ☐   play the guitar ☐   collect things ☐
send text messages ☐   go shopping ☐   listen to music ☐   surf the web ☐

Presentation

2 **Warm up** **Look at** *Poppy's world* **on page 53 and answer the questions.**
Who is in photo A? What has Poppy got? Who is in photo B? What has Jack got?

3 ⊙ **2.22** **Listen and read the photo story. Are the sentences true (*T*) or false (*F*)?**
Correct the false sentences.

1 Emma's dad collects old pop records. F
2 David's mum reads in her free time.
3 Jack doesn't play football.
4 Emma surfs the web and sends text messages.
5 Jack plays the electric guitar in his free time.
6 David doesn't do his homework after school.

Language focus

• **Do you surf** the web?
  Yes, I do.
• **Does he write** emails?
  No, he doesn't.
• **Do they watch** TV?
  Yes, they do.
• But **they don't watch** TV on Saturday.

4 **Read** *Language focus*. **Then work in pairs and answer the questionnaire.**
A Do you surf the web?   B Yes, I do.

5 **Complete the questionnaire about you. Mark your answers with a tick (✓).**

Do you love or hate computers?

Do you ...?	yes	no
read books?		
read magazines?		
write letters?		
play a musical instrument?		
meet your friends?		
play board games with friends?		

Get 1 for every 'yes' answer.
Score ☐

Do you ...?	yes	no
surf the web?		
download music?		
play computer games?		
send text messages?		
write emails?		
write a blog?		

Get 2 for every 'yes' answer.
Score ☐

SCORE

0 – 6   Oh dear! Do you live in the twenty-first century?
7 – 12 Fantastic! You like computers but you also spend
        time with your friends.
13 – 18 You love computers! But do you see your friends?

A ⊙ 2.22 **I love my mobile. It's got a video camera. I film my friends. I ask lots of questions!**

Poppy What do your parents do in their free time, David?
David Well, my dad collects old pop records.
Poppy Old pop records?
David Yeah. He likes The Beatles and The Rolling Stones! And my mum reads newspapers and books and magazines.
Poppy Do they watch TV?
David Yes, they do. But they don't watch TV on Saturday.
Poppy What do you do after school?
David I do my homework!
Poppy Me too! Do you surf the web, Emma?
Emma Yes, I do. I go shopping, too. And I send text messages to my friends … like you!
Poppy What about Jack? Does he play computer games?
Emma No, he doesn't.
Poppy Does he listen to music?
Emma Yes, he does. But Jack's got a special hobby.
Poppy What's that?
Emma Follow me … to the garage!

B Jack doesn't watch DVDs in his free time. And he doesn't play football. He plays the electric guitar. And he's fantastic!

Your space Talking about your interests

6 Complete the sentences.
My favourite free time activity is ¹……………………………… .
At the weekend I ²……………………………… .
In the evening I ³……………………………… .

7 Work in pairs and compare your sentences with your partner.
A At the weekend I go shopping.
B I don't. I play football.

Chat zone
Me too!
… like you!
What about Jack?
Follow me …

Present simple – negative

1 (Circle) the correct form of the verb. Use the table to help you.

full form			short form		
I you	do not		I you	don't	
he she it	does not	work.	he she it	doesn't	work.
we you they	do not		we you they	don't	

1 They (**don't**) / **doesn't** have English lessons on Friday.

2 She **don't** / **doesn't** like horror films.

3 I **don't** / **doesn't** get up early on Sunday.

4 James **doesn't** / **don't** like bananas.

5 Luis **doesn't** / **don't** surf the web before school.

6 We **doesn't** / **don't** see our cousins every day.

2 ◉ **2.23** Cross (✗) the activities Archie doesn't do on Saturdays.

go to a football match

play with my pets

read a newspaper

read a book

eat fast food

do my homework

take photos

see my grandparents

help my mum

go to the park

play a musical instrument

3 ✎ Write sentences about the things Archie doesn't do on Saturday.

He doesn't play with his pets.

4 ☼ Work in pairs. Talk about activities you don't do on Saturday.

I don't read a newspaper.

Present simple – questions and short answers

5 Complete the conversation with the present simple. Use the table to help you.

.... it bite?

No, it ....

questions			short answers			
Do	I you		Yes,	I do. you do.	No,	I don't. you don't.
Does	he she it	work?	Yes,	he she does. it	No,	he she doesn't. it
Do	we you they		Yes,	we you do. they	No,	we you don't. they

6 Complete the conversation with Archie. Use the words below.

do don't does doesn't

Lisa: .... you get up early on Sunday?

Archie: No, I ....

Lisa: .... your dad read a newspaper?

Archie: Yes, he .... In fact, he reads two!

Lisa: .... your mum cook a big Sunday lunch?

Archie: No, she .... My dad cooks it!

Lisa: .... your parents watch TV in the evening?

Archie: Yes, they ....

Lisa: .... you do your homework in the evening?

Archie: Yes, I .... It's terrible!

7 ✎ **Write questions and true answers.**

1 you / like English lessons?
Do you like English lessons?
Yes, I do.

2 your mother / cook your dinner?

3 your school / start at half past eight?

4 you and your friends / walk to school together?

5 you and your family / have coffee for breakfast?

6 you / go to the park on Saturdays?

7 your grandparents / surf the web?

8 🗨 **Work in pairs. Ask your partner the questions from Exercise 7. Do you give the same answers?**

9 **Complete the clocks with the times you do these activities.**

get up
have breakfast
have lunch
go to school
go home
have dinner
do your homework

10 🗨 **Work in pairs. Ask and answer questions with your partner.**

A What time do you have breakfast?
B I have breakfast at seven o'clock in the morning.

⟩ **Language check page 139**

 Your words ⊞ **4B**

have

have *breakfast*

have *lunch*

have *dinner*

have *a shower*

have *a party*

before and after

I have a shower at 7 am. I have breakfast at 7:30 am.
↓
*I have a shower **before** I have breakfast.*
*I have breakfast **after** I have a shower.*

I finish school at 3:30 pm. I go to football practice at 4 pm.
↓
*I finish school **before** I go to football practice.*
*I go to football practice **after** I finish school.*

11 🗨 **Work in pairs. Tell your partner about you.**

1 I have breakfast at ....

2 I have lunch at ....

3 I have dinner at ....

12 🗨 **Compare your days.**

I have breakfast before you!

Reading

1 Warm up Look at the pictures and answer the questions.

Where do the people work? What do you think they do in their jobs?

It's My Job
– and I love it!

We ask three people about their job

A circus performer

I work in a circus. I'm a trapeze artist – I walk on the high wire. I travel all over the world – to Australia, Japan, the USA. It's very exciting! I live in a big circus family. I get up early and practise every day. I work Monday to Friday, and at the weekend, too! I spend lots of time away from home. I don't see my real family for weeks! But I love my job.
Rosa Sanchez

A zoo keeper

Guess what? I love animals! At the zoo, I prepare food for the animals and I clean their living spaces. I work about eight hours a day. I don't only work with animals, I work with people, too. I answer their questions. My job is great, but I don't like one thing ... I wear a uniform – and I don't like uniforms!
Alexia Georgiou

A games tester

I play computer games ... for my job! I work 10 to 12 hours a day. I work in a big team in an office. It's fun – but it's also a bit boring. Why? Because I test the same game again and again! After work, I go home and sleep (I'm very tired!) or talk to my work friends about our favourite hobby. That's right – computer games!
Tomasz Nowak

2 ⊙ **2.25** **Read and listen. Then complete the sentences with the people's names.**

1 _Alexia_ works with animals.
2 _____ works at the weekend.
3 _____ works with lots of other people.
4 _____ doesn't see her family for weeks.
5 _____ uses a computer.
6 _____ doesn't like her uniform.

3 Work in pairs. Ask and answer the questions.

Whose jobs do you like / don't you like? Who has got the best job?

Vocabulary • Jobs

4 **2.26** **Match the words with the pictures. Then listen and check.**

doctor [10]   bus driver ☐   shop assistant ☐   teacher ☐   police officer ☐
mechanic ☐   hairdresser ☐   office worker ☐   farmer ☐   actor ☐

5 **Copy and complete the table. Then check your answers with a partner.
You can use some jobs more than once.**

Who … ?			
wears a uniform	works outside	works at night	uses a computer
bus driver			

Listening and speaking

6 **2.27** **Listen and write the jobs.**

1 a hairdresser

7 **Work in groups and play *What's my job?*
One student mimes, your group says the job.**

A Are you a doctor?   B No, I'm not.
A Are you an artist?   B Yes, I am.

Writing

8 **Choose one of the jobs from Exercise 4. Ask and answer the
questions with a partner. What is your partner's job?**

- What time do you start / finish work?
- Do you drive / use a computer every day?
- Do you wear a uniform or special clothes?
- Do you work with other people / with animals / outside / at night?

9 **Write a description of one of the jobs.**

I'm a hairdresser. I start work at …

Study skills

Noticing words
- We often use certain words in pairs. Write them in your *Vocabulary notebook*.
  watch + TV
  do + homework
  get + washed

5A Can you swim?

Grammar
can – positive and negative forms, questions and short answers • adverbs of manner

Functions
talking about ability • talking about how well you do things

Vocabulary • Sport

1 🔘 **2.30** **Match the words with the pictures. Then listen and check.**

basketball [6] cycling [ ] football [ ] tennis [ ] volleyball [ ]
gymnastics [ ] karate [ ] rugby [ ] running [ ] swimming [ ]

1   2   3   4   5

6   7   8   9   10

Presentation

2 **Warm up Look at *Poppy's world* on page 59 and answer the questions.**
Who is in the playground? How many apples has Poppy got?

3 🔘 **2.31** **Listen to the photo story. Are the sentences true (*T*) or false (*F*)? Correct the false sentences.**
1 Jack and Emma can play football very well. F   They can play tennis very well.
2 David can swim quite well.
3 Amy can run, swim and play football.
4 Poppy can play basketball very well.
5 Poppy can't swim at all.
6 Poppy can't juggle.

4 🔘 **2.32** **Listen to Alex and tick (✓) the sports he can do.**
do karate [ ] play football [ ] cycle [ ]
swim [ ] juggle [ ] skateboard [ ]

5 **Read *Language focus*. Write sentences about what Alex can and can't do.**
1 He can't do karate. 2 He can play football.

Language focus

• I **can** juggle.
• Jack and Emma **can** play tennis.
• David **can** swim.
• I **can't** play football.
• **Can you** play football? **Yes**, I **can**. / **No**, I **can't**.

✓✓ I can juggle **very well**.
✓ I can play basketball **quite well**.
✗✗ I **can't** swim **at all**.

A 2.31 **All my friends like sport – and there's a sports competition at school next week. Jack and Emma can play tennis very well. David can swim quite well. And Amy is brilliant. She can run, swim and play football!**

Amy	Hey, Poppy. Do you want to be in our sports team?
Poppy	Er … yeah, OK.
Amy	Great. Can you play football?
Poppy	No, I can't. I can't play football.
Amy	What about basketball?
Poppy	I can play basketball quite well. But I'm not very tall.
Amy	That's true. Can you run very well?
Poppy	No, I can't.
Amy	Erm … Can you swim?
Poppy	No, I can't. I can't swim at all!
Amy	Can you do any sport, Poppy?

B **I've got a secret skill. I'm good at juggling!**

Poppy	I can juggle.
Amy	Can you?
Poppy	Yes, I can. Watch.
Amy	Wow, Poppy. You can juggle very well! You're amazing!
Poppy	Thanks. Am I in the team?
Amy	Erm … no. Sorry. There isn't a juggling competition!

Your space   Talking about sport

6 **Work in pairs. Ask and answer questions about sport.**

A Can you play tennis?
B Yes, I can. I can play tennis very well. What about you?
A No, I can't. I can't play tennis at all.

7 **Tell the class about your partner.**

Kyle can play tennis very well, but I can't.

Chat zone

That's true.
You're amazing!
Sorry.

can – positive and negative

1 Read and (circle) the correct verbs. Use the table to help you.

1 Zak *can / can't* cook.
2 Robopet *can / can't* skateboard.
3 Max and Lara *can / can't* juggle.

	positive	negative	
I you he she it we you they	can	can't	dance.

2 ✎ Write sentences. Use *can / can't*.

1 you / cook ✗   You can't cook.
2 my teacher / play the guitar ✓
3 I / swim ✓
4 Our dog / sing ✗
5 My friend and I / play volleyball ✓
6 They / speak French ✗
7 Harry and Mark / do karate ✓
8 My Dad / ride a bike ✗

3 ✿ Work in pairs. Tell your partner four things you can do and four things you can't do.

I can play tennis. I can't sing.

can – questions and short answers

questions		short answers				
Can	I you he she it we you they sing?	Yes,	I you he she it we you they can.	No,	I you he she it we you they can't

Soundbite

(can / can't)

◎ **2.33** Listen and repeat.
1 Can you run?   Yes, I can.
2 Can you swim?   No, I can't.
3 I can run, but I can't swim.

4 Look at the table and complete the conversations with *can* or *can't*.

Gran	✓ use a computer surf the web send an email
	✗ play computer games download music
Grandad	✓ drive cook
	✗ use a computer use a mobile phone

Lucy: Gran, ¹ _can_ you use a computer?
Gran: Yes, I ² _____ . I ³ _____ surf the web and I ⁴ _____ send emails, too.
Lucy: Cool. And ⁵ _____ you play computer games?
Gran: No, I ⁶ _____ . And I ⁷ _____ download music. Can you teach me?
Lucy: Of course. What about Grandad?
Gran: Oh, Grandad ⁸ _____ use a computer.
Lucy: ⁹ _____ he use a mobile phone?
Gran: No, he ¹⁰ _____ . But he ¹¹ _____ drive. And he ¹² _____ cook. That's useful!

5 ☆ **Work in pairs. Tick (✓) the things you can do. Then talk to your partner and tick (✓) the things he / she can do.**

A Can you swim under water?
B Yes, I can.

CAN YOU...?

swim under water ☐

play the guitar ☐

ride a horse ☐

do karate ☐

say the alphabet backwards ☐

juggle three balls ☐

stand on one leg ☐

sing a song in English ☐

row a boat ☐

do a handstand ☐

Score
1 – 3 Oh dear! Try a new skill.
4 – 6 Not bad!
7 – 10 Wow! Take a break.

6 ☆ **Report to the class.**
Ben can play the guitar.

Adverbs of manner

✓	quite well	✗	not very well
✓ ✓	very well	✗ ✗	not at all

7 🖉 **Tick (✓) two things you can do and cross (✗) two things you can't do. Then write about how you can do them.**

I can play tennis quite well.
I can't ride a bike very well.

ride a bike   play tennis   take photos
cook   skate   paint   dance   do Maths
play the piano   run   write poetry

8 ☆ **Work in pairs. Tell your partner your sentences. Are your sentences different?**

Get it right!

Use the correct word order for questions:
Can you sing?   NOT   ~~You can sing?~~

5B I love running

Grammar
present simple • *like, love, hate + -ing* • imperatives

Functions
talking about likes and dislikes

Vocabulary • Activities

1 **○ 2.34 Match the words with the pictures in the questionnaire on page 63. Write the letters, then listen and check.**

walking [G]   staying in bed [ ]   reading books and magazines [ ]
doing puzzles [ ]   playing computer games [ ] playing chess [ ]
singing [ ]   playing ball games [ ]

Presentation

2 **Do the questionnaire *Are you fit and active?* Count your *a* and *b* answers. Then read *Score*.**

3 **Work in groups. Talk about your answers together.**
A I love running.
B I love running, too.
C I don't like running. I like staying in bed!

4 **Tell the class about your group's answers.**
Three people in our group love running. One person loves doing puzzles.

5 **Read *Language focus*. Complete the sentences with things you like and don't like doing.**

☺☺ I love _____ and _____ .

☺ I like _____ and _____ .

☹ I don't like _____ or _____ .

☹☹ I hate _____ and _____ .

Language focus

• I **love watching** sport.
• I **like playing** ball games.
• I **don't like flying**.
• I **hate getting up**.

6 **Work in pairs. Ask and answer questions about your free time.**
A What do you like doing in your free time?
B I like riding my bike. And I love watching TV.
A Do you like running?
B No, I don't.
A What do you hate doing?
B I hate staying in bed.

62 Unit 5 Keep fit!

Are you fit and active?

Tick (✔) the best answers for you.

1 I love …
a running ☐
b reading ☐

2 In the morning I hate …
a staying in bed ☐
b getting up ☐

3 What do you like doing at the weekend?

a		*b*	
walking	☐	doing puzzles	☐
playing ball games	☐	reading books and magazines	☐
tidying my room	☐	playing chess	☐
singing	☐	playing computer games	☐

4 I love …
a doing sport ☐
b watching sport ☐

5 I do something active for …
a about an hour a day ☐
b about ten minutes a day ☐

6 I like …
a cycling ☐
b going by car ☐

Score

Mostly a's: You are a sporting hero! Don't forget to rest!
Mostly b's: Oh dear! Don't sit in that chair. Get up! Do a sport!

Your space   My favourite activities

7 Write about what you like and don't like doing in your free time. Use *like, love, don't like* and *hate*.

I love listening to music. My favourite singer is
Pixie Lott. I like swimming. I go to the swimming pool
on Wednesdays. But I don't like playing football!

like, love, hate + -ing

1 **Complete the sentence with the verbs.**

> sleeping   waking up

It's spring and Bruno the bear wakes up after the winter.

He loves ...., but he hates ....!

2 **Write true sentences with the *-ing* form.**

> I *like sleeping late at the weekend.*
> **1** I like ....
> **2** I don't like ....
> **3** I love ....
> **4** I hate ....
> **5** My mum loves ....
> ....
> **6** My mum doesn't like ....
> ....
> **7** My dad doesn't like ....
> ....
> **8** My best friend loves ....
> ....

3 ☆ **Work in pairs. Tell your partner your sentences.**

4 ◉ **2.35** **Complete the table.**

love = ✓✓ like = ✓ not like = ✗ hate = ✗✗

	listen to rock music	do sports	take photos	play chess
Amy				
Martin				
Jessica				
Lee and Joe				

Soundbite

/ɪŋ/

◉ **2.36** **Listen and repeat.**
writing listening speaking sending
giving shopping studying

5 ✎ **Write sentences about the people.**

Amy *loves listening to rock music and doing sports. She doesn't like taking photos. She hates playing chess.*

6 ☆ **Work in pairs. Ask your partner questions about people in their family.**

> play chess   watch old films   cook
>
> do crosswords   read magazines
>
> listen to rock music   take photos

A Does your dad like watching old films?
B Yes, he does.

Imperatives

7 **Complete the signs.**

1 _Don't take_ photos in the museum. (not take)

2 _____ food on this bus. (not eat)

3 _____ English! (speak)

4 Please _____ in the library. (not talk)

5 _____ your mp3 players. (not use)

6 _____ paper in this bin, please. (put)

7 _____ this hat in cold water. (wash)

8 Please _____ the animals. (not feed)

Language check page 140

do and make

do

do sport

do your homework
do an exercise
do a test

make

make a cake

make a noise
make a mess
make a mistake

8 **Complete the sentences with _do_ or _make_.**

1 I can _make_ cakes. They're delicious!
2 I _____ my homework after school.
3 Shhh. Don't _____ a noise in the cinema!
4 My mum _____ lots of sport.
5 My brother _____ a terrible mess in his bedroom.
6 **Teacher:** _____ Exercise five with your partner.
7 Adam _____ mistakes in Maths.
8 We _____ a vocabulary test every week.

Reading and speaking

1 **Warm up Read the webpage quickly and answer the questions.**
What is *Sports4you*? Who can go there?

2 **Read the webpage again. Are the sentences true (*T*) or false (*F*)?**
Correct the false sentences.
  1 You meet your teachers at 9 am. T
  2 You do sport in the morning for three hours.
  3 You go home for lunch.
  4 In the afternoon you do three different sports.
  5 In the evening you go home after dinner.
  6 On Friday there is a talent show.
  7 On the last day there are races and games.
  8 You can stay in bed all day at *Sports4you*.

3 **Work in pairs. Imagine you are at the sports camp. Choose two**
sports. Talk about your sports with a partner.
My two sports are volleyball and swimming. I can swim quite well.
But I can't play volleyball.

http://yourspace.cambridge.org/

SPORTS4YOU
A SUMMER CAMP FOR ALL SPORTS FANS

Home · Info · About Us · Contact

SPORTS4YOU is especially for 11–14 year-olds.
▷ Try a new sport. ▷ Learn new skills. ▷ Get fit.

Have fun and make new friends!

A TYPICAL DAY
⚽ The day starts at 9 am. You meet your teachers and get ready for sport! It's like an Olympic Village for teenagers!
⚽ In the morning you choose a sport. And you do it for three hours. But there is lots of time to watch and learn.
⚽ At lunchtime you can eat and chat with your new friends.
⚽ In the afternoon you do a different sport. Or you can try wall climbing, horse riding or mountain biking.
⚽ At the end of the day you are tired. But there's a nice dinner or a barbecue. And time to be with your friends!
⚽ After dinner there's lots of fun! A game show on Monday, a talent show on Tuesday, a film on Wednesday, and a treasure hunt on Thursday.

THE LAST DAY
⚽ Friday is *Sports4you* Olympics day! There are lots of races and games. It's time to show your new skills. Can your team win?
⚽ In the evening there's a disco with all your friends!

Listening

4   ⊙ **2.38**   **Match the sentence parts. Then listen and check.**

Weird animal facts

1 Gorillas   **a** can't close their eyes.
2 Ostriches   **b** can stay under water for 30 minutes.
3 Snakes   **c** can't jump.
4 Snails   **d** can sleep for three years.
5 Whales   **e** can run at 70 km an hour.
6 Elephants   **f** can sing for 20 minutes.
7 Hippos   **g** can learn 1,000 words.
8 Grey parrots   **h** can't swim.

Writing

5   **Work in pairs. Ask your partner about their free time. Make notes. Can you … ?**

play football   swim   dance   ride a bike   ride a horse
skate   ski   play volleyball   climb trees   sing
play the guitar   paint   draw   play the piano

6   **Write about your partner.**

> Oleg can play football. He can't ride a horse or a bike. He can't play the guitar or the piano. But he can swim very well. He can paint and draw, too.

Study skills

Making notes
• When you make notes, only write the important facts.
A Anja, can you play football?
B Yes, I can.
A And can you play volleyball?
B No, I can't.

Anja
can play football
can't play volleyball

➤ **Communication page 122**   ➤ **Your Space Web Zone**   Keep fit!   **Unit 5**

6A I always walk to school

Grammar
adverbs of frequency • present simple – question words • prepositions of time

Functions
talking about daily routine and habits

Vocabulary • School subjects

1 ⊙ **2.41** **Match the words with the pictures. Then listen and check.**

Maths [2]   Religious Education (RE) [ ]   Geography [ ]   Music [ ]
Art [ ]   Physical Education (PE) [ ]   Drama [ ]   English [ ]   History [ ]
Science [ ]   Information and Communication Technology (ICT) [ ]   Languages [ ]

Presentation

2 ⊙ **2.42** **Listen and complete Lauren's timetable on page 69. Do you study the same subjects?**

3 **Work in pairs. Ask and answer questions about your school timetable.**
A What lessons do you have on Monday morning?   **B** Maths and Art.

4 ⊙ **2.43** **Read and listen to Lauren's project. Are the sentences true (*T*) or false (*F*)? Correct the false sentences.**

1 Lauren goes to a primary school called Lakeside Community School. F
Lauren goes to a secondary school called Lakeside Community School.
2 Year 7 is the second year of secondary school.
3 She often plays computer games on the school computers.
4 She usually goes home for lunch.
5 She never eats meat for her main meal at school.
6 She walks to school.
7 She always goes to Homework Club after school.
8 She enjoys drumming.

5 **Read *Language focus* and <u>underline</u> adverbs of frequency in Lauren's project.**

Language focus

100% –	– always
	– usually
	– often
	– sometimes
	– not often
0% –	– never

2.43

My School
by Lauren

Hi there. This project is about my school. I go to Lakeside Community School. I'm in Year 7 – the first year of secondary school. I like my new school. I've got lots of new friends. There are about 600 boys and girls at my school, so it's quite small.

The teachers are nice and I like the fun experiments in Science! The school has got a great sports centre and lots of computers. I often go to the computer room at lunchtime and play computer games with my friends.

I always have lunch at school. I like the food – I usually have a hot lunch and a piece of fruit. I never eat fish. I don't like it, so on Friday I have the vegetarian option.

I always walk to school with my friends. But I don't always come home at 3:15 when school finishes. I sometimes go to Homework Club after school and I do my homework there. I can ask the teacher for help. And I go to the Drumming group on Wednesday. It's cool – I love drumming.

My new school is different from my old school. But I like it here.

Here is my school timetable:

	Monday	Tuesday	Wednesday	Thursday	Friday
9:10 Lesson 1	Maths			ICT	English
10:10	Break				
10:25 Lesson 2		Maths			
11:25 Lesson 3	Geography	Maths	History		
12:25	Lunch				
1:20 Lesson 4	Science				
2:20 Lesson 5		English	Maths		German

Your space   Talking about your daily routine

6 Write four true sentences and one false sentence about your daily routine.

I always do my homework. I sometimes go to the cinema.

7 Work in pairs. Read your sentences to your partner. Which is your partner's false sentence?

Adverbs of frequency

1 (Circle) the correct adverb of frequency. Use the table to help you.

You win again! You *always* / *never* win!

always	▮▮▮▮▮▮▮▮▮▮	100%
usually	▮▮▮▮▮▮▮▮	80–99%
often	▮▮▮▮▮▮	60–80%
sometimes	▮▮▮	20–60%
not often	▮▮	1–20%
never		0%

2 ✍ **Put the words in the correct order to make sentences.**

1 seven o'clock / get up / we / usually / at
   We usually get up at seven o'clock.
2 at school / lunch / they / have / often
3 my parents / to the shops / drive / never
4 writes / sometimes / Joe / letters
5 eat / often / apples / Isabel / doesn't
6 don't / usually / TV / my parents / watch

3 ✍ **Complete the Factfile about you.**

FACTFILE

1 I *usually get up* early.
2 I *don't often play* computer games.
3 I .... (watch) TV.
4 I .... (walk) to school.
5 I .... (help) my parents at home.
6 I .... (send) text messages.
7 My best friend .... (ride) a bike.

4  **Work in pairs. Compare your sentences with your partner.**

Get it right!

Remember to put the adverb of frequency in the correct place:
I sometimes have pizza for lunch.
NOT ~~I have sometimes pizza for lunch.~~
My friends never visit me.
NOT ~~My friends visit me never.~~

Prepositions of time

at	five o'clock midnight	on	14th June 6th May
at	night	in	January
on	Wednesday Monday morning Friday afternoon	in	the morning the afternoon the evening the summer

5 **Complete the sentences with the prepositions from the table.**

1 We go on holiday _in_ August.
2 They don't watch TV .... the evening.
3 I don't go to school .... Sunday.
4 I get up .... half past six.
5 My birthday is .... 7th September.
6 I have a piano lesson .... Friday.

6  **Work in pairs. Ask and answer questions.**

When do you go on holiday?
In August.

go   do
be   play
watch   have

holiday   TV
birthday
dinner   football
bed   school

Question words and present simple

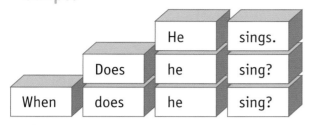

	He	sings.
Does	he	sing?
When	does	he	sing?

7 ○ **2.44 Match the questions and answers. Listen and check.**

1 Where do you have lunch? e
2 How do you go to school?
3 What do you do on Friday evening?
4 What time do your classes finish?
5 Which do you prefer, pasta or pizza?
6 Why do you always wear pink?

a I play football.
b Because I like it.
c Pizza!
d By bus.
e In the school canteen.
f Half past three.

8 ☆ **Work in pairs. Ask and answer the questions from Exercise 7.**

9 ☆ **Ask and answer questions with these words.**

A What do your parents eat for breakfast?
B Cereal.

10 ○ **2.45 Complete the conversation with the verbs. Listen and check.**

Sam: Hi, my name's Sam.
Anita: Hello, Sam. I'm Anita.
Sam: ¹ Do you go (go) to Westgate School?
Anita: No, I ² _____ . I ³ _____ (not live) in London.
Sam: Where ⁴ _____ you _____ (live)?
Anita: I ⁵ _____ in York. But my friend Melissa ⁶ _____ (go) to Westgate School. ⁷ _____ you _____ (know) her?
Sam: Yes, I ⁸ _____ . She's my sister's best friend!
Anita: Really? That's amazing!
Sam: ⁹ _____ you _____ (come) from York?
Anita: Yes. My parents ¹⁰ _____ (work) there.
Sam: ¹¹ _____ you _____ (like) York?
Anita: Yeah. It's a great place. I ¹² _____ (love) the shops and the museums.

what   when   where   who   why

do   does

you   your best friend   your English classes
your parents

eat for breakfast   go on holiday   go to bed
watch on TV   get up   surf the web
finish   go to school   go swimming
start
do your homework   listen to music
wear jeans   watch cartoons

Grammar
must – positive and negative forms • object pronouns

Functions
talking about obligation • talking about possession

Presentation

1 **Warm up Look at *Poppy's world* on page 73 and answer the questions.**
Where is Poppy? Who can you see in the photos? What has Poppy got in photo A?

2 🔘 **2.46 Listen to the photo story and answer the questions.**
1 What does Miss Naylor take from Poppy?
2 Where is Poppy's Maths homework?
3 Where is Miss Naylor's mobile phone?
4 Whose mobile phone rings during the lesson?

3 **Find and <u>underline</u> the sentences from *Language focus* in the photo story. Can you find more sentences?**

Language focus

• You **must bring** it to the lesson.
• You **mustn't use** your mobile phone at school.
• I **mustn't forget** the school rules.

Vocabulary • School rules

4 🔘 **2.47 Match the expressions with the pictures. Then listen and check.**
use your mobile phone ☐   run in the corridor ☐   be polite ☐
drop litter ☐   be quiet ☐   wear school uniform ☐   do your homework ☐
eat or drink in the classroom ☐   chew gum ☐   listen to music ☐ 1

1 ☒   2 ☐   3 ☐   4 ☐   5 ☐

6 ☐   7 ☐   8 ☐ Sshhh   9 ☐   10 ☐ Please, Thank you.

5 🔘 **2.48 Listen to the rules. Tick (✓) the things you must do, and cross (✗) the things you mustn't do in Exercise 4.**

6 **Complete the rules for Greenwood School.**

You must ...	You mustn't ...
do your homework.	listen to music.

7 **Work in pairs. Say a number from 1 to 10. Your partner says the rule from Exercise 4.**
A Number five.
B You mustn't eat or drink in the classroom.

A ◉ **2.46 I like school … but I'm not a perfect student!**

Teacher What's that noise? Poppy?

Poppy Erm … it's my mobile, Miss. I've got a text message.

Teacher Do you know the school rules, Poppy?

Poppy I'm not sure, Miss Naylor.

Teacher Well, you mustn't use your mobile phone at school. Is that clear?

Poppy Yes, Miss. I mustn't use my mobile at school.

Teacher That's right. Now give me your phone, Poppy. You can have it after the lesson.

Poppy Thank you, Miss.

Teacher Now, open your books. Where's your Maths homework, Poppy?

Poppy It's at home, Miss.

Teacher You must bring it to the lesson.

Poppy Yes, Miss. Sorry, Miss.

I mustn't forget the school rules. And I must remember my homework!

B **Ten minutes later …**

Teacher OK, do Exercise 3. You mustn't talk to your partner …
I don't believe it! Whose mobile phone is that?

Poppy It isn't mine, Miss!

Teacher Then whose mobile is it?

David Erm … I think it's yours, Miss.

Teacher What? Oh, yes. Sorry. Now, do Exercise 3.

David Yes, Miss.

Chat zone

I'm not sure.
That's right.
I don't believe it!

Your space Talking about rules

8 **What are your school rules? Write a list.**

We must do our homework.

9 **Work in pairs. Talk to your partner about your list. Is your information the same or different?**

must – positive and negative

1 Match the sentences with the pictures. Then (circle) the correct verbs. Use the table to help you.

 1 ☐

 2 ☐

a I'm very tired and slow. I *must / mustn't* get new batteries.

b Get down! You *must / mustn't* sleep on the bed.

I you he she it	**must**	follow the school rules.
we you they	**mustn't**	eat lots of sweets.

2 Complete the sentences with *must* or *mustn't*.

1 You <u>mustn't take</u> photos. (take)

2 You .... here. (cycle)

3 You .... right. (turn)

4 You .... quiet in the library. (be)

5 You .... on the grass. (walk)

6 You .... litter in the bin. (put)

3 ◉ **2.49** Listen and tick (✓) or cross (✗) the rules.

House Rules
☐ help in the kitchen
☐ play computer games after eight
☐ listen to music after ten
☐ do your homework
☐ use your mobile phone at the table
☐ drop your clothes on the floor
☐ watch TV in the morning
☐ learn these rules!

4 ☆ Work in pairs. Tell your partner about the rules in your house.

I must make my bed.
I mustn't play loud music.
I must do my homework before supper.
I mustn't play games on my dad's computer.

5 ✎ Write six rules for your ideal school.

My ideal school rules!

The teachers must give sweets to the children.
You mustn't do homework at the weekend.
You must send text messages during lessons.

....
....
....
....
....
....
....

Object pronouns

subject pronouns	object pronouns
I	me
you	you
he	him
she	her
it	it
we	us
you	you
they	them

6 Complete the sentences.

1 We're going to the shops. Come with ....
2 Here's my new mobile phone. Do you like .... ?
3 Jessica Alba is in that film. Do you like .... ?
4 Do you like cartoons? I watch .... all the time.
5 That's my pen. Give it to .... !
6 You're great, Mum! I love ....
7 Orlando Bloom's a brilliant actor. I like ....

➡ **Language check page 140**

go

go + to

go to work

go to school   *go to* bed

go + to the

go to the cinema

go to the doctor's   *go to the* supermarket

go

go shopping

go home   **Go** away!

7 Read the sentences. Circle the correct words.

1 I *go to school* / *go to the school* at eight o'clock in the morning.
2 Grace *goes to shopping* / *goes shopping* on Tuesday afternoon.
3 I *go to bed* / *go to the bed* at ten o'clock at night.
4 My dad *goes to work* / *goes to the work* very early in the morning.
5 We always *go to cinema* / *go to the cinema* on Saturday evening.
6 I *go to home* / *go home* with my friends after school.

Vocabulary • Clothes

1 🎧 **2.51** **Match the words with the pictures. Then listen and check.**

trainers [10]   shirt [ ]   trousers [ ]   tie [ ]   jacket [ ]   sweatshirt [ ]
shoes [ ]   skirt [ ]   dress [ ]   T-shirt [ ]   sweater [ ]   coat [ ]

1
2
3
4
5
6
7
8
9
10
11
12

2 🎧 **2.52** **Listen to Kirsty. What clothes does she wear at school? What clothes does she wear at the weekend? Make notes.**

Reading

3 **Warm up** Read the notice on page 77 quickly and match the photos with the clubs.

4 🎧 **2.53** **Listen and read the notice again. Then answer the questions.**

1 What time does the theatre group finish?
2 Which club meets on Wednesday and Friday?
3 Where can you paint and take photos?
4 Where can you learn circus skills?
5 What club is on Tuesday at 5 pm.?

Listening and speaking

5 🎧 **2.54** **Listen to Mizuki and Nathan. Complete the table.**

Name	Mizuki	Nathan
From	Tokyo, Japan	Sydney, ...
School days		
School starts / finishes		
Favourite subjects		
School clubs		
School uniform		

6 **Work in pairs. Imagine you are Mizuki or Nathan. Interview your partner.**
What …? Where …? What days …? What time …? Do you …?

Change your life – join a club! ⊙ 2.53

It's quarter past three. It's time to go home, right? Wrong! This is your chance to join one of our fantastic after-school clubs. So don't watch TV or play computer games at home. Look at the great things you can do here … at school!

Art studio **A**

Come to the studio on Thursday after school. You can do lots of brilliant artwork. Learn to make masks, paint a picture, take photos – be creative!

Theatre group **B**

Do you want to be an actor? Go to Hollywood? Well, you can be an actor in a school play. You can also learn circus skills. Monday from 4 to 5 pm.

Orchestra **C**

Do you play an instrument? Can you read music? We want new musicians for the orchestra. It's fun and we play in concerts, too! Tuesday at 5 pm.

Jazz dance **D**

We love dancing! And jazz dancing is really good fun. Get fit and move your body. Classes on Wednesday and Friday.

Science club **E**

Science can be cool. Do great experiments and learn exciting new things about the world. We always meet on Thursday at 4 pm.

School magazine **F**

Who makes the school magazine? You! Talk to people, write, design, think of new ideas … or check the spelling!

Writing

7 Write an email to Katja. Describe your school.

> Hi Katja,
> This is an email about my school.
> We go to school from ¹_____ to ²_____ . (*days of the week*)
> School starts at ³_____ and finishes at ⁴_____ . (*time*)
> We study ⁵_____ . (*subjects*)
> My favourite subject is ⁶_____ . These are our school clubs: ⁷_____ .
> I go to ⁸_____ (*school club*) or I play ⁹_____ . (*sport*)
> Bye for now,
>
> (*your name*)

▶ Communication page 123   ▶ Your Space Web Zone

7A There isn't any ice cream

Grammar
countable and uncountable
nouns • a / an, some / any
Functions
talking about quantity

Vocabulary • Food

1 ○ **2.58 Match the words with the pictures. Then listen and check.**

eggs 6   apples ☐   grapes ☐   ice cream ☐   biscuits ☐   melons ☐   oranges ☐
chicken ☐   cheese ☐   chocolate ☐   bananas ☐   ham ☐   tomatoes ☐   crisps ☐

2 **Work in pairs. Talk about the food in the pictures.**
   A I love tomatoes.   **B** I don't eat ham.   **A** I don't like bananas.

Presentation

3 ○ **2.59 Read and listen to *Poppy's world* on page 79. Then circle the correct answer.**
   1 What do the friends want to do?   **a** have a picnic   **b** play football
   2 What do they do?   **a** they go to the park   **b** they stay at home

4 ○ **2.59 Listen to the photo story again. Tick (✓) the food and drink in the picnic.**

Our picnic

sandwiches ✓   bananas   crisps   ice cream   water
fruit juice   chocolate   chicken   biscuits   tomatoes
apples   melon   grapes   cola

5 ○ **2.60 Read *Language focus* and complete the conversation with *some* or *any*.
   Then listen and check.**
   After the picnic …
   Mum   There's ¹ some food left!
   Poppy Yes, there are ² .... sandwiches left.
   Mum   But I see there aren't ³ .... crisps left!
              Is there ⁴ .... fruit left?
   Poppy There aren't ⁵ .... bananas.
   Mum   And is there ⁶ .... chocolate left?
   David No, there isn't ⁷ .... chocolate, Mrs Young.
   Mum   Well, I've got a treat! There's ⁸ .... ice cream
              in the freezer.
   All   Hurray!

Language focus
- We've got **some** sandwiches.
- There's **some** fruit juice.
- We haven't got **any** grapes.
- There isn't **any** ice cream.
- Is there **any** chocolate?
- Are there **any** crisps?
- And there's **a** melon.

A ● 2.59 **It's the weekend and it's the perfect time for a picnic in the park!**

Amy	Have we got all the food?
Poppy	Let's check. We've got some sandwiches …
David	Is there any chicken? It's great for picnics.
Poppy	Yes, David, we've got some chicken.
Emma	And we've got some tomatoes.
David	Are there any crisps? I love crisps.
Poppy	Yes, there are. And there's a melon.
Jack	Have we got any bananas?
Emma	We've got five bananas. But we haven't got any grapes.
Amy	What about fruit juice?
Emma	There's some fruit juice and there's some water.
Poppy	OK. Let's go!

B **David has got a problem.**

David	Wait a minute! Is there any chocolate?
Emma	Yes, there is. Don't worry.
David	But there isn't any ice cream.
Poppy	David! It's a picnic.
David	Only joking.
Jack	What's that noise?
Poppy	Oh no! Rain!

C **The weather isn't always great in the summer. But you can always have a picnic!**

Jack	Great picnic, Poppy!
Poppy	Thanks, Jack.
David	Yeah, nice chocolate, too.

Chat zone

Let's go!
Wait a minute!
Only joking.

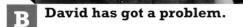

Your space   Planning a picnic

6   **Work in groups. Choose six things for your picnic. Write about what is / isn't on your list.**

There's some chocolate, but there aren't any apples.
There isn't any chicken, but there is some cheese.

some or *any*, *a* or *an*

1 Complete the cartoon with *some* or *any*. Use the table to help you.

Some or any
There is (There's) **some** water.
There are **some** crisps.
There isn't **any** water.
There aren't **any** crisps.
Is there **any** water?
Are there **any** crisps?

Zak: Have you got .... water?

Man: No, I haven't. But I've got
.... oranges. Have you got
.... money?

Zak: No, I haven't!

2 Put the food words in the correct group.

sandwiches melons ice cream
crisps apples water chicken
meat cheese eggs biscuits
chocolate tomatoes bananas
fruit juice cola grapes

countable	uncountable
sandwiches	ice cream

Get it right!

These words are uncountable:
information NOT ~~informations~~
homework NOT ~~homeworks~~
money NOT ~~moneys~~

3 Write the correct form of the words.

1 Have you got two _TVs_ .... ? (TV)

2 I've got some great .... on my mp3 player. (music)

3 Can you give me some .... ? (information)

4 Give me some .... (paper)

5 I've got some .... (idea)

6 I can sing lots of .... (song)

7 I've got some .... (homework)

8 She has got blonde .... (hair)

4 Write *some* or *any*, *a* or *an*.

1 I've got _a_ .... cheese sandwich.

2 There's .... water in the bottle.

3 Are there .... tomatoes in the salad?

4 There isn't .... milk.

5 Have you got .... chocolate?

6 There are .... delicious biscuits.

7 There's .... fruit juice here.

8 There's .... banana too.

Soundbite

/ɪ/ /iː/

🔘 **3.02** Listen and repeat the chant.

I like fish and chips and chicken and chips
Crisps and chocolate biscuits.
I like cheese and peas and sweets and beans
Pizzas and chocolate ice cream!

5 Work in pairs. Look at the fridge and ask and answer questions.

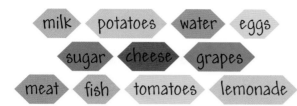

milk potatoes water eggs

sugar cheese grapes

meat fish tomatoes lemonade

A Is there any milk?
B Yes, there is.
A Are there any potatoes?
B No, there aren't.

6 Draw a fridge with food and drink in it.

7 Work in pairs. Tell your partner about your fridge. Listen and draw your partner's fridge.

8 3.03 Circle 'yes' or 'no'.

1 photos / on Dan's mobile   yes | no
2 money / on the table   yes | no
3 films / on TV tonight   yes | no
4 homework / tonight   yes | no
5 sugar / in my coffee   yes | no
6 people / in the room   yes | no

9 Write the questions and short answers.

Are there any photos on Dan's mobile?
Yes, there are.

10 Look at the picture and write sentences. Use the words in the box.

pens dictionaries books fruit
photos postcards water comics
pencils chocolate

A Are there any pens?
B Yes, there are.

11 Write a description of your ideal desk.

How much fruit do you eat?

Grammar
How much? How many?
• *lots, not much, not many*

Functions
talking about quantity

Vocabulary • Food

1 Work in groups. Add the words to the spidergrams. Can you think of any more?

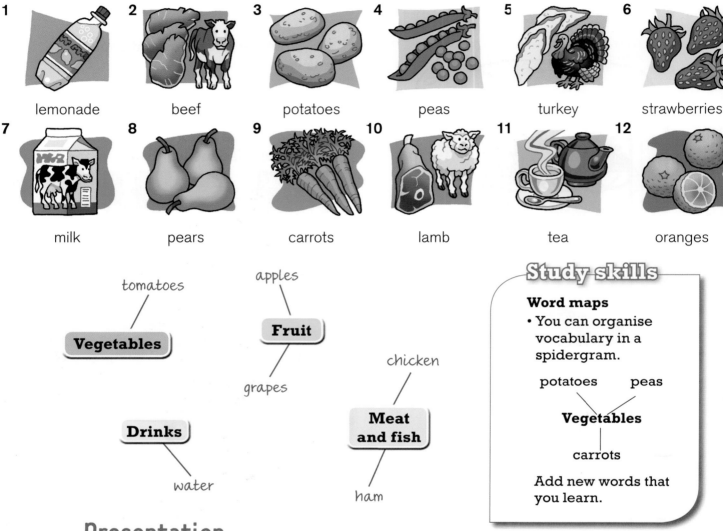

1 lemonade
2 beef
3 potatoes
4 peas
5 turkey
6 strawberries
7 milk
8 pears
9 carrots
10 lamb
11 tea
12 oranges

tomatoes
apples
Vegetables
Fruit
grapes
chicken
Drinks
Meat and fish
water
ham

Study skills

Word maps
• You can organise vocabulary in a spidergram.

potatoes   peas

Vegetables

carrots

Add new words that you learn.

Presentation

2 **Warm up** Look at the photos of food on page 83 and answer the question.
What can you see?

3 🔘 **3.04** Listen and work out David's score.

4 Read *Language focus* and <u>underline</u> other examples of *How much …?* and *How many …?* in the questionnaire.

5 Work in pairs. Ask and answer the questions from the questionnaire. Then work out your scores.

Language focus

• **How much** fruit do you eat?
• **How much** water do you drink?
• **How many** biscuits do you eat?

Are you a healthy hero or a junk food fan?

3.04 **What do you eat and drink in a week? Write your score.**

a lot 3   quite a lot 2
not much / many 1   none 0

Group 1

How much …

fish do you eat? ☐

fruit do you eat? ☐

salad do you eat? ☐

water do you drink? ☐

fruit juice do you drink? ☐

milk do you drink? ☐

How many …

nuts do you eat? ☐

vegetables do you eat? ☐

a lot 0   quite a lot 1
not much / many 2   none 3

Group 2

How much …

chocolate do you eat? ☐

ice cream do you eat? ☐

cola do you drink? ☐

How many …

biscuits do you eat? ☐

packets of crisps
do you eat? ☐

cakes do you eat? ☐

sweets do you eat? ☐

hamburgers do you eat? ☐

Score

31 – 48 Wow! You're a healthy hero. Well done!

16 – 30 OK. But be careful with junk food.

**0 – 15 Oh dear! You're a junk food fan.
You must change your diet.**

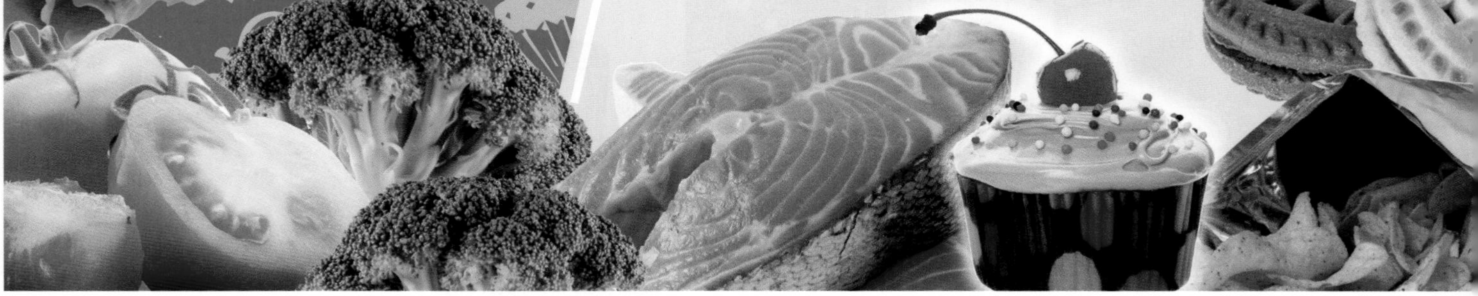

Your space   My favourite meal

6   **Write sentences about your favourite food.**

My favourite meal is fish, chips and peas.
My mum makes a fantastic chocolate cake.
I love pizza with egg at the restaurant near my home.

much / many / lots

1 Complete the questions with *much* or *many*. Match them with the pictures. Use the table to help.

uncountable	countable
How much water is there?	How many apples are there?

a How .... food has Zak got?
b How .... pets has Max got?
c How .... homework have Max and Lara got?
d How .... birthday cards has Zak got?

2 Match the answers with the questions in Exercise 1.

1 He's got lots. ☐
2 He hasn't got much. ☐
3 He hasn't got many. ☐
4 They've got lots. ☐

3 🖎 Look at the pictures and write sentences with *lots of / not much / not many*.

1 There are lots of books.

2 .... water.

3 .... sweets.

4 .... money.

5 .... luggage.

6 .... keys.

7 .... orange juice.

8 .... people.

4 ☁ Work in pairs. Ask and answer about the things in Exercise 3.

A How many books are there?
B There are lots.

5 🔘 **3.05** Listen and number the shopping trolleys 1 to 4.

6 Complete the questionnaire with *How much* or *How many*.

What do you do in a typical week?

1	How many	websites do you visit?
2		music do you listen to?
3		text messages do you send?
4		computer games do you play?
5		homework do you do?
6		comics do you read?
7		TV do you watch?
8		money do you spend on sweets?

7 ☆ **Work in pairs. Ask and answer questions from Exercise 6.**

A How many websites do you visit?
B Not many.
A How much music do you listen to?
B Lots.

➡ Language check page 141

and, but, too

Swoosh

Wonder Girl is very strong. Wonder Girl can fly.
*Wonder Girl is very strong **and** she can fly.*

Big Guy eats spinach.   *Big Guy doesn't eat hamburgers.*

*Big Guy eats spinach, **but** he doesn't eat hamburgers.*

Gecko Boy drives a car.   *Gecko Boy climbs buildings.*

*Gecko Boy drives a car. He climbs buildings, **too**.*

8 **Complete the sentences with *and*, *but* or *too*.**

1 I can run, *but* I can't swim.
2 Owen studies German. He studies French, ...
3 There's fruit juice .... milk in the fridge.
4 I like chocolate, ... I don't like sweets.
5 They play tennis .... they go running.
6 Lara loves drawing. She loves writing, ...

7C Skills

Reading

1 ⊙ **3.07** **Warm up** Match the words with the photos from the magazine article on page 87. Then listen and check.

tomato pasta [8]   burger and chips ☐   jacket potato ☐   cakes ☐
apple pie ☐   sandwiches and a banana ☐   fish and chips ☐   chicken curry ☐

2 **Read the article quickly and match the food with the people.**

1 chicken curry – Azra

3 **Read the article again and write the letters.**
Who …

1 has a packed lunch? ☐ ☐   3 doesn't eat meat? ☐   5 likes chicken? ☐ ☐
2 likes soup? ☐   4 has chips? ☐ ☐   6 eats fruit? ☐ ☐

Listening and speaking

4 ⊙ **3.08** **Some students talk about lunch at school. Number the trays in the order you hear them.**

☐    ☐    ☐    ☐

5 **Work in pairs. Ask and answer questions.**

What do you usually have for lunch?   What's your favourite fruit?
What's your favourite sandwich?   What's your favourite school meal?

Writing

6 **Keep a food diary for two days. Write what you eat and drink. Start today. Include breakfast, lunch and dinner, and don't forget snacks!**

> My food and drink diary
> Monday 12th May
> Breakfast
> orange juice   toast   fruit

What's for lunch?

School students in the UK take a packed lunch (usually sandwiches) or they have a school lunch. Let's talk to some students from Leeds about their school lunches.

a I love school lunch. They've got meat and vegetables and salads. But I usually have a burger and chips. Chips are great!
Harry

b I take a packed lunch. I make my sandwiches in the morning. I always have a yoghurt and a banana, too. Oh, and I sometimes have a packet of crisps.
George

c I like soup. My favourite is vegetable soup. But I sometimes have a jacket potato with cheese. I have some fruit, too. Usually an apple.
Eve

d I don't really like my school dinners. They aren't very good. But the chicken is OK and I like the desserts. Especially apple pie!
Stefan

e My mum makes my packed lunch. And she usually makes some little cakes, too.
Alexandra

f In my religion I can't eat some types of meat. But my school serves special meals. And I love their chicken curry!
Azra

g I'm a vegetarian – I don't eat meat. So I usually have a salad. My school also does amazing tomato pasta, with lots of cheese. Yummy!
Shannon

h They do good food in my school. I love the pizza. And on Friday I always have fish and chips.
Anthony

Here's a British school menu from 120 years ago!

1 PENNY DINNER: MEAT AND VEGETABLES
¼ PENNY DINNER: SOUP AND BREAD
FREE DINNER: HOT CHOCOLATE

Communication page 124   Your Space Web Zone

Grammar
present continuous – positive and negative forms

Functions
talking about actions in progress

Presentation

1 **Warm up** Look at the photos of places on page 89. Match the photos with these words:

a knight on a horse ☐   a big wheel ☐   a giraffe ☐   an exciting ride ☐

2 **Read the text messages on page 89. Are the sentences true (*T*) or false (*F*)?**
Correct the false sentences.

1 Lara is sitting at home. F   *Lara is sitting in a café.*
2 Alton Towers is near Birmingham.
3 Oliver is standing next to a giraffe.
4 Crackers is eating her normal lunch.
5 Alicia is in London with her friends.
6 She is standing in the London Eye.
7 Ahmed is sitting next to his dad.
8 His mother and sister are watching the knights.

Vocabulary • Animals

3 **3.11** **Match the photos with the words. Then listen and check.**

an elephant ☐3☐   a koala ☐   a tortoise ☐   horses ☐
a tiger ☐   bears ☐   a bat ☐   kangaroos ☐

4 Read *Language focus*. Work in pairs. Talk about what the animals are doing in the photos. Use these verbs:

sleep   eat   swim   fly   fight   play   wash   run

The tortoise is eating.
The bears are playing.

5 Work in pairs. Think of an animal and talk about what it *isn't* doing. Can your partner guess the animal?

A It isn't eating.
B Is it the elephant?
A No, it isn't.
B Is it the bat?
A Yes, it is.

Language focus

- **I'm writing** this message to you!
- **We're looking** at Big Ben.
- She **isn't having** lunch.
- My mum and my sister **aren't watching** the knights.

A great day out

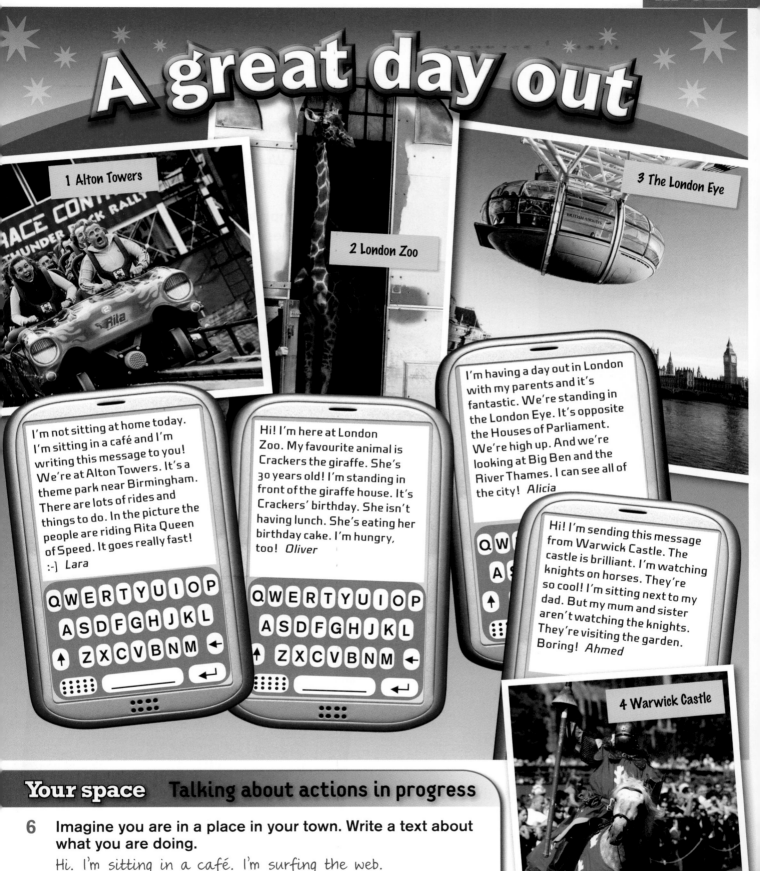

1 Alton Towers

2 London Zoo

3 The London Eye

I'm not sitting at home today. I'm sitting in a café and I'm writing this message to you! We're at Alton Towers. It's a theme park near Birmingham. There are lots of rides and things to do. In the picture the people are riding Rita Queen of Speed. It goes really fast! :-] *Lara*

Hi! I'm here at London Zoo. My favourite animal is Crackers the giraffe. She's 30 years old! I'm standing in front of the giraffe house. It's Crackers' birthday. She isn't having lunch. She's eating her birthday cake. I'm hungry, too! *Oliver*

I'm having a day out in London with my parents and it's fantastic. We're standing in the London Eye. It's opposite the Houses of Parliament. We're high up. And we're looking at Big Ben and the River Thames. I can see all of the city! *Alicia*

Hi! I'm sending this message from Warwick Castle. The castle is brilliant. I'm watching knights on horses. They're so cool! I'm sitting next to my dad. But my mum and sister aren't watching the knights. They're visiting the garden. Boring! *Ahmed*

4 Warwick Castle

Your space Talking about actions in progress

6 **Imagine you are in a place in your town. Write a text about what you are doing.**

Hi. I'm sitting in a café. I'm surfing the web.
I'm not eating a cake, but I'm eating an ice cream.
My sister is reading a magazine.

Present continuous – positive

1 Complete the sentence. Use the table to help you.

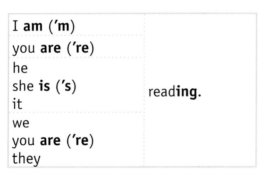

I .... writing text messages and Max .... reading them.

I **am** ('m)	
you **are** ('re)	
he	
she **is** ('s)	read**ing**.
it	
we	
you **are** ('re)	
they	

Present continuous spelling rules		
wear	→	wear**ing**
write	→	writ**ing**
dance	→	danc**ing**
stop	→	stopp**ing**
travel	→	travell**ing**
study	→	study**ing**

2 Write the *-ing* form of these verbs.

liking

like say walk eat drive
stay ride take run
win sit make have

3 🔘 **3.12** Listen and number the activities.

play computer games ☐ watch TV ☐
listen to music ☐ eat pizza ☐
talk on the phone ☐ ride a bike ☐
do homework ☐ play football ☐

4 ✏️ Write about each activity.

She's playing football.

5 Complete the sentences. Use the present continuous.

We ¹ *'re having* (have) a great time. Anna and Sarah ² .... (dance). Abi ³ .... (take) photos. David and Karim ⁴ .... (swim). Eddie's dog ⁵ .... (run). Joel ⁶ .... (play) the guitar. Georgia ⁷ .... (sing) a pop song. I ⁸ .... (talk) on the phone.

Get it right!

Remember to use the correct form of the verb:

I'm going home. NOT ~~I'm go home.~~

Present continuous – negative

6 **Complete the sentences. Use the table to help.**

I	am not ('m not)	
you	are not (aren't)	
he she it	is not (isn't)	dancing.
we you they	are not (aren't)	

1 I .... to the teacher. (not listen)
2 Jane .... her glasses. (not wear)
3 The cat isn't hungry. He .... his food. (not eat)
4 My mum .... today. (not work)
5 We .... in the pool today. The water is cold. (not swim)
6 They .... football now. (not play)

7 📝 **Look at the picture and write sentences about Simon.**

1 <u>He's sitting on his bed.</u>
   (sit on his bed)
2 <u>He isn't eating.</u>
   (eat)
3 ....
   (play a computer game)
4 ....
   (talk on the phone)
5 ....
   (read his books)
6 ....
   (listen to music)
7 ....
   (play his guitar)

8 **Close your books and try to remember the picture.**

9 💬 **Work in pairs. Look at the picture. What are the children wearing?**

A She's wearing a ...
B He's wearing ...

10 💬 **Work in pairs. Say what you and your partner are wearing today.**

> I'm wearing a blue T-shirt and my partner's wearing ...

> I'm wearing ... and my partner's wearing ...

Grammar
present continuous – questions and short answers • present continuous or present simple

Functions
talking about the weather

Vocabulary • Weather

1 🔘 **3.13 Match the sentences with the pictures. Then listen and check.**

It's sunny. [5]   It's snowing. ☐   It's cloudy. ☐   It's windy. ☐

It's foggy. ☐   It's raining. ☐   It's hot. ☐   It's cool. ☐

2 **Work in pairs. Ask and answer questions about the weather.**
A What's the weather like today?
B It's cloudy and cool. And it's a bit windy.

Presentation

3 **Warm up Look at *Poppy's world* on page 93 and answer the questions.**
Where are Poppy and her friends in the first photo?
What are they doing? Where are they in the second photo?

4 🔘 **3.14 Listen and read the photo story. Answer the questions.**

1 What does Poppy usually do on Saturday?
2 What's the weather like in Wales?
3 What's David doing?
4 What's Emma doing?
5 Why can't the girls sleep?
6 What's the weather like at night?

5 **Read *Language focus*. Think of four people you know. What are they doing now?**

brother   sister   mum   dad   uncle   aunt
best friend   teacher

6 **Work in pairs. Ask and answer questions about the people you know.**

A What's your aunt doing now?
B I don't know. What's your brother doing now?
A He's working in an office.

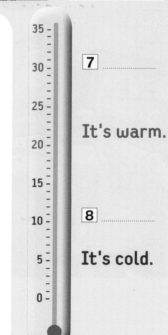

7 .... **It's warm.**

8 .... **It's cold.**

Language focus

- **What are** you **doing**?
- **Where are** you **calling** from?
- **Are** you **having** a good time?
  Yes, I **am**.
- **Is** David **helping** you?
  No, he **isn't**.
- **Are** you **sleeping**?
  No, I'm **not**.

A ⊙ **3.14** **I usually go shopping on Saturday. But today is different. I'm staying in the countryside with friends. We're camping! I must call Jack and tell him.**

Jack	Hi, Poppy! Where are you calling from?
Poppy	I'm in Wales! What's the weather like at home?
Jack	It's raining. It's horrible!
Poppy	Poor you! It's warm and sunny here.
Jack	Are you having a good time?
Poppy	Yes, I am.
Jack	What are you doing?
Poppy	Well, I'm talking to you … and we're putting up our tent!
Jack	Is David helping you?
Poppy	No, he isn't. He's putting up the boys' tent. I'm working with Amy.
Jack	What's Emma doing?
Poppy	She's cooking our lunch.
Jack	Great!
Poppy	It's fantastic here, Jack. It's the best thing ever!

B **It's late at night. I usually sleep a lot but I'm not sleeping now!**

Poppy	Are you sleeping?
Amy	No, I'm not. I can't. I'm so cold.
Emma	I'm cold, too.
Poppy	Me too. It's really windy outside. Listen.
Emma	Oh no! Look at our tent!
Amy	It's falling down!
Poppy	Help!

Your space Keeping a weather diary

7 **Keep a diary for a week. Write about the weather each day.**

Monday 9th: Today it's snowing and very cold.
Tuesday 10th: Today it isn't snowing, but it's very cold.
Wednesday 11th: …

Chat zone
Poor you!
It's the best thing ever!
Help!

Present continuous – questions and short answers

1 Complete the cartoon conversation. Use the table to help you.

.... you cleaning your room?

Yes, I ....

Am I		Yes, I am.	No, I'm not.
Are you		Yes, you are.	No, you aren't.
Is he she it	singing?	Yes, she is. he it	No, she isn't. he it
Are we you they		Yes, you are. we they	No, you aren't. we they

2 ⊙ **3.15** Match the questions with the answers. Listen and check.

1 Are you listening to me? d
2 What are you wearing?
3 Where are you calling from?
4 Is Josh watching football on TV?
5 What are you doing?
6 Is Lizzie eating chocolate?
7 Why are you running?
8 What are Oscar and Lucy doing?

a No, she isn't.
b We're making a sandwich.
c They're tidying their rooms.
d Yes, I am.
e I'm late for school!
f My new jacket.
g Yes, he is.
h Outside the cinema.

3 ☆ **Work in groups. Mime an activity to your classmates. Can they guess?**

A Are you playing a computer game?
B No, I'm not.
A Are you sending a text message?
B Yes, I am.

> ride a bike   play football   play tennis
> do homework   play a computer game
> read a magazine   send a text message
> walk in the countryside   write an email
> go shopping   sleep   do a crossword puzzle
> watch a tennis match   play chess

Present continuous or present simple?

4 ✎ **Look at the table and write two sentences for each person.**

Henry usually plays the violin. Today he is playing the electric guitar.

		usually	today
Henry		play the violin	play the electric guitar
Alice		work in a library	ski
Alex		ride a bike	ride a horse
Julia		have a sandwich for lunch	eat in a restaurant
Jade		wear a T-shirt and jeans	wear a dress

5 ☆ **Work in pairs. Ask and answer questions about Exercise 4.**

A What does Henry usually do?
B He usually plays the violin.

6 ✎ **Look at the picture. Write questions and answers. Use the present simple or the present continuous.**

1 What is George doing?
   He's listening to music.
2 What game does Lexi play ?
   She plays tennis.
3 Where is Lexi sitting?
   ....
4 ....?
   He's wearing a T-shirt and jeans.
5 Who is Lexi's favourite actor?
   ....
6 ....?
   No, he isn't eating. He's drinking.
7 ....?
   Yes. They've got a dog called Spot.
8 ....?
   He's playing with a tennis ball.
9 What is Lexi doing?
   ....
10 Are George and Lexi doing their homework?
   ....

➡ **Language check page 141**

feelings

hungry

thirsty

tired

happy

sad

angry

scared

excited

bored

interested

I'm hungry. <u>NOT</u> ~~I've hungry.~~
I'm feeling happy. <u>NOT</u> ~~I'm being happy.~~

7 Choose a feeling for these situations.

1 when you win a prize happy
2 at a pop concert ....
3 before going to a restaurant ....
4 on a hot day ....
5 at the end of a long day ....
6 during a long lesson ....
7 after your team loses a match ....

Vocabulary • Places

1 🔘 **3.17 Match the words with the pictures. Then listen and check. Which of these places can you find in your area?**

the countryside [4]   a mountain [ ]   a forest [ ]   a hill [ ]

a port [ ]   a river [ ]   the sea [ ]   a lake [ ]

Reading and listening

2 Read Jamie's webpage quickly on page 97. Match the headings with the paragraphs.

Sport [ ]   The city [1]   Museums [ ]   Boat trips [ ]

Shopping [ ]   Music [ ]   The people [ ]

3 Read the webpage again. Are the sentences true (T) or false (F)? Correct the false sentences.

1 The river in Liverpool is called the Mersey. *T*
2 It's in the south of England.
3 There is one cathedral in Liverpool.
4 The Beatles are from Liverpool.
5 Liverpool has got one football team.
6 You can take trips on the river.

4 🔘 **3.18 Where are the people? Listen and write their names next to the places.**

1 the Beatles Story ....
2 the Maritime Museum ....
3 the Duckmarine ....

Writing

5 Write about your town. Then tell your partner your sentences. Is your information the same or different?

New York is a fantastic city. It is famous for fashion, food and art.

Study skills

Finding key words
The key words can help you understand what a text is about.

*There is a **ferry trip** on the **River Mersey** – it's fun. But I love the **Yellow Duckmarine**. It's a **bus and a boat**! It goes on **streets** and in **water**! I love it.*

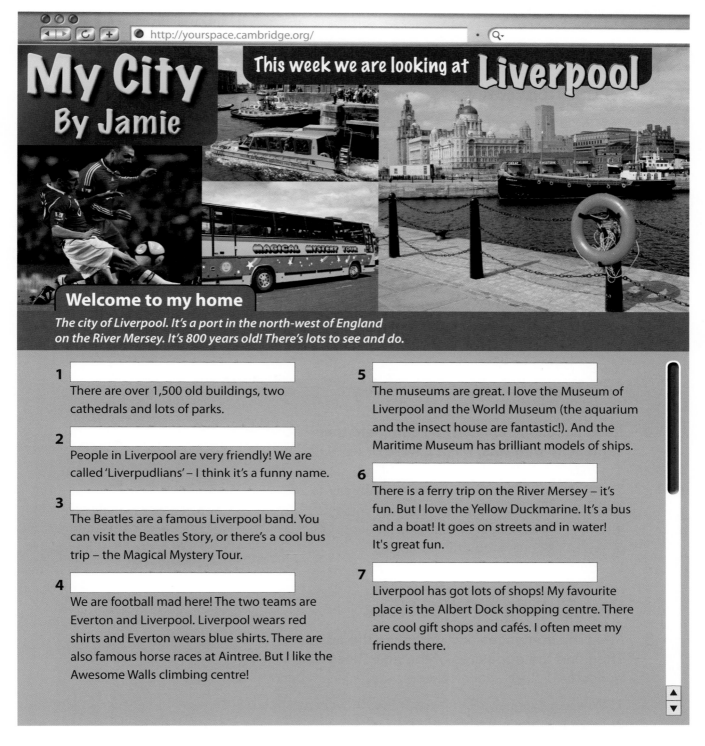

Welcome to my home

The city of Liverpool. It's a port in the north-west of England on the River Mersey. It's 800 years old! There's lots to see and do.

1 [ ]
There are over 1,500 old buildings, two cathedrals and lots of parks.

2 [ ]
People in Liverpool are very friendly! We are called 'Liverpudlians' – I think it's a funny name.

3 [ ]
The Beatles are a famous Liverpool band. You can visit the Beatles Story, or there's a cool bus trip – the Magical Mystery Tour.

4 [ ]
We are football mad here! The two teams are Everton and Liverpool. Liverpool wears red shirts and Everton wears blue shirts. There are also famous horse races at Aintree. But I like the Awesome Walls climbing centre!

5 [ ]
The museums are great. I love the Museum of Liverpool and the World Museum (the aquarium and the insect house are fantastic!). And the Maritime Museum has brilliant models of ships.

6 [ ]
There is a ferry trip on the River Mersey – it's fun. But I love the Yellow Duckmarine. It's a bus and a boat! It goes on streets and in water! It's great fun.

7 [ ]
Liverpool has got lots of shops! My favourite place is the Albert Dock shopping centre. There are cool gift shops and cafés. I often meet my friends there.

Speaking

6 Work in groups. Two students describe a town or a place. The third student must guess the place.

A It's very big. It's old. There are lots of museums. There's a big river.
B The people speak French. It's famous for the Eiffel Tower.
C Is it Paris?
A and B Yes, it is!

Presentation

1 **Warm up** **Answer the questions.**

Where is Poppy? Why do you think she isn't at school? What is she doing?

2 ⊙ **3.21** **Read and listen to *Poppy's world* on page 99.**
Match the photos with the text messages.

3 ⊙ **3.21** **Listen again. Then complete the table.**

	Saturday	Sunday
Poppy	She was at home in bed.	She was
David	He was in London at the Science Museum.	He was
Amy	She was	She was
Emma and her mum	They were	They were
Jack, Charlie and their dad	They were	They were

4 **Read *Language focus*. Then complete the**
sentences with *was*, *wasn't*, *were* or *weren't*.

1 I _was_ at the cinema last night. (✓)
2 Sarah and Abi _____ at work yesterday. (✓)
3 _____ you at the swimming pool yesterday?
4 I _____ at school on Monday morning. (✗)
5 _____ Louis tired after football?
6 You _____ at home last night. (✗)

Vocabulary • Adjectives

5 **Read the sentences and <u>underline</u> the adjectives.**
Then find the opposites of the adjectives below.

wonderful   quiet   poor   ~~cheap~~   ugly   safe   boring   difficult

1 What an <u>expensive</u> TV! It costs €2,000! cheap
2 I love this dress. It's beautiful.
3 This party is very noisy. I want to go home.
4 These questions are easy. I know all the answers.
5 That restaurant is terrible. Don't go there!
6 I'm reading an interesting book about pandas.
7 Don't cross the road without looking. It's dangerous.
8 That man has a lot of money. He's very rich.

6 **Read *Poppy's world* again and find four abbreviations. Can you guess**
what they mean?

GR8 = great

Language focus

- I **was** in London on Saturday.
- We **were** in Manchester.
- It **wasn't** very interesting.
- We **weren't** at home last weekend.
- **Were** you in bed all weekend?
- Where **were** you at the weekend?

🔘 **3.21** **It's Monday and I'm sitting in my bedroom. I feel terrible!**

9.27 AM
Cancel new message Send
To: David, Amy, Emma
Subject: Hi!

Hi guys
I'm sorry I'm not in school with you today. I was in bed with a cold on Saturday and Sunday. What about you? Where were you at the weekend?
Tell me your news!
Poppy

1
9.52 AM
Cancel new message Send
To: Poppy
Subject: re: Hi!

Hi Poppy
Oh dear! Your weekend wasn't very good. Poor you! I was in London on Saturday at the Science Museum. There were some GR8 machines. Then on Sunday my family and I were at a car race. It was noisy but it was fun.
C U soon!
David

2
10.02 AM
Cancel new message Send
To: Poppy
Subject: re: Hi!

Hi there, Poppy
Were you in bed all weekend? You poor thing! I was at home all weekend, too. My aunt has got a new baby. We were with the baby all day. No music. No TV. Just baby talk. Boring! Get well soon.
Luv
Amy

3
10.14 AM
Cancel new message Send
To: Poppy
Subject: re: Hi!

Hi Poppy
How R U? We weren't at home last weekend. We were in Manchester! On Saturday I was at the shops with my mum. Jack, Charlie and my dad were at an exhibition. It wasn't very interesting! On Sunday we were in the car all day. It was a long journey!
C U 2MORO?
Emma

a

b

c

Your space Talking about where you were

7 **Work in pairs. Talk about where you were.**
on Sunday evening   on Saturday morning
at 7:00 this morning   yesterday afternoon

A Where were you at seven o'clock this morning?
B I was at home in the kitchen.

8 **Tell the class about your partner.**
Pia was at home at seven o'clock this morning.

Chat zone
Boring!
Hi guys.
Get well soon.

Language space

Past simple verb *be* — positive and negative

1 **Match the sentences with the pictures. Use the table to help you.**

1 We were on the London Eye.
2 Zak was a bit scared!
3 On Saturday I was in London with Lara, Max and Robopet.

	positive	negative
I	was	was not (wasn't)
you	were	were not (weren't)
he she it	was	was not (wasn't)
we you they	were	were not (weren't)

2 **Put the time expressions in order.**

1 last night   2 yesterday

last night   on Saturday   last month

three days ago   yesterday

two weeks ago   in 2004

3 **Change the sentences to the past simple.**

1 I'm tired today.
  I was tired yesterday.
2 I'm not at my desk.
3 It's my birthday today.
4 We aren't at school today.
5 It is hot and sunny today.
6 They aren't rich.
7 They are at the sports centre today.
8 They are in Paris today.
9 She isn't in the sports hall.
10 You are happy today.

4 **Complete the email from Ali. Use *was* or *were*.**

Hi Jasmine

How R U? Last weekend ¹ was   great   . We
² .... in New York with my uncle. His apartment is
near Central Park. On Saturday we ³ .... at the Natural
History Museum. It ⁴ .... near my uncle's apartment.
It ⁵ .... very interesting and the dinosaur skeletons
⁶ .... fun! On Sunday there ⁷ .... a surprise
— the Statue of Liberty! There ⁸ .... 354 steps to the
top. We ⁹ .... at the top of the
statue's head! The view ¹⁰ ....
fantastic!

C U after the holidays

Ali

5 **3.22** **Listen and check.**

Get it right!

Use the correct form of the verb:
You were in Brighton yesterday.
NOT ~~You was in Brighton yesterday.~~
They weren't at my party on Saturday.
NOT ~~They wasn't at my party on Saturday.~~

Past simple verb *be* – questions and short answers

6 Complete the conversation. Use the table to help you.

Police officer: .... you at home last night?

Man: No, I ....

Police officer: .... you in another person's house last night?

Man: Yes, I ....

Police officer: Where .... you last night?

Man: I .... at a fancy dress party!

question		positive	negative
Was	I ...?	Yes, I was.	No, I wasn't.
Were	you ...?	Yes, you were.	No, you weren't.
Was	he she ...? it	Yes, she was.	No, she wasn't.
Were	we you ...? they	Yes, you were.	No, you weren't.

7 ⊙ **3.23** Listen and ⟨circle⟩ *yes* or *no*.

	Yes No	Yes No
Sam	at the swimming pool	at the cinema
Olivia	at home	at the shops
Joe and Billy	at the circus	at the zoo
Gabriel and Maria	at the pizza restaurant	at the youth club

8 ✎ Write sentences about the friends.

Sam wasn't at the swimming pool. He was at the cinema.

9 ☆ Work in pairs. Ask and answer questions about yesterday.

> tired   busy   happy   sad
> bored   excited   angry   relaxed

A Were you tired yesterday?
B Yes, I was.
A Were you happy yesterday?
B No, I wasn't.

10 ☆ Work in pairs. Ask and answer questions.

Where	was were	you your parents your best friend your brother your sister your teacher	at eight o'clock? this morning? last night? yesterday? on Sunday? on Saturday? three days ago?

A Where was your sister on Saturday?
B She was at her friend's house.
A Where was your teacher last night?
B I don't know!

Grammar
past simple regular verbs – positive form

Functions
talking about past events

Vocabulary • Transport

1 ⊙ **3.24** **Match the words with the pictures. Then listen and check.**

car ☐4   ship ☐   yacht ☐   plane ☐   motorbike ☐
bicycle ☐   bus ☐   train ☐   helicopter ☐   space ship ☐

2 **Put the words in the spidergrams.**

on the ground

in the air

on the water

car

Presentation

3 **Warm up** **Look at the photos and the map on page 103. Answer the questions.**
What do you think the article is about?
What places can you see on the map?

4 ⊙ **3.25** **Read and listen to the article about Michael Perham. Then complete the sentences.**
1 Michael was .... old when he sailed across the Atlantic Ocean.
2 It's .... kilometres from Gibraltar to Antigua.
3 His yacht was .... metres long.
4 Michael's journey was .... days long.
5 His father sailed .... kilometres behind Michael's boat.

5 **Read the article again. Tick (✓) Michael's activities.**
cycle ☐   play the drums ☐   sail ☐   cook ☐   study ☐   play the guitar ☐
play computer games ☐   juggle ☐   watch TV ☐   film ☐   see his friends ☐

6 **Read** *Language focus*. **Then** (circle) **the past simple of these verbs in the article.**
decide sail finish stay cook film ask study play juggle miss enjoy arrive

Language focus

- His journey **started** in Gibraltar in November.
- Michael's father **followed** him.
- They **talked** on a special mobile phone.
- In his free time he **played** the guitar.
- They **travelled** home in a plane.

Atlantic Wonderboy

Atlantic Ocean

Pacific Ocean

Michael Perham started sailing when he was only six!

It's 5,600 kilometres from Gibraltar in the Mediterranean to Antigua in the Caribbean. The journey goes across the Atlantic Ocean, and people usually travel by plane or ship. But 14-year-old Michael Perham decided to go by yacht! And he sailed on his own in his small yacht *Cheeky Monkey*. It was only eight metres long.

His six-week journey started in Gibraltar in November 2006, and it finished 47 days later in Antigua on the 3rd January 2007. Michael's father followed him in a different yacht, but he stayed three kilometres behind Michael. They only talked on a special mobile phone.

It's a dangerous journey and there's a lot to do in a yacht. So Michael worked very hard. He sailed and he cooked all his food. And he filmed his journey with a video camera. His teachers asked him to do homework so he studied, too! But in his free time he played the guitar and juggled. Michael missed his family. And he missed his computer games and his drums.

Michael enjoyed his adventure. But when he arrived in Antigua, he was happy: 'It feels fantastic being back on land.' He and his father travelled home in a plane ... not a yacht!

Your space   Writing about the past

7 **Write about what you and your family did last night. Choose from these activities.**

study   cook a meal   watch TV   work   play computer games
play football   talk to friends   visit my grandparents
help my parents   surf the web   listen to music

Last night my dad worked on his computer.
I watched TV last night.
I studied English before dinner.

Past simple positive – regular verbs

1 📖 Read and complete the email. Use the table to help you.

Hi Lara

We're finally in New York! But it was a long journey. Our satnav was terrible! We ¹ _started_ in London last month! First Robopet and I ² _____ (travel) by space ship to Australia. We ³ _____ (walk) across the desert on Tuesday. Then on Wednesday we ⁴ _____ (climb) the Himalayas and on Thursday we ⁵ _____ (sail) to China. On Friday we ⁶ _____ (stay) in India. And on Saturday we ⁷ _____ (arrive) in New York!

See you soon

Zak and Robopet

Past simple spelling rules		
arrive	→	arrived
live	→	lived
study	→	studied
marry	→	married
stop	→	stopped
plan	→	planned
open	→	opened
offer	→	offered
⚠ travel	→	travelled ⚠

2 Write the past simple forms of these verbs.

like   talk   call   live   wash
paint   carry   use   touch
close   stop   open   love
look   dance

🔊 **3.26** Listen and repeat the verbs.
1 talked   finished
2 arrived   played
3 started   decided

🔊 **3.27** Listen to the verbs. Are they 1, 2 or 3?

sailed 2   watched   travelled   stayed
followed   worked   lived   cooked   studied

3 Complete the sentences with the past simple of the verbs.

1 Emily _decided_ (decide) to buy a hat.
2 We _____ (listen) to music all day!
3 Harry _____ (watch) a great film!
4 My parents _____ (cook) an Indian meal on Sunday.
5 Last week I _____ (visit) a museum.
6 My brother's train _____ (arrive) three hours late!
7 I _____ (phone) my friend Sameer yesterday.

4 📖 Read and complete Alice's report on the school website. Use the past simple of the verbs in brackets.

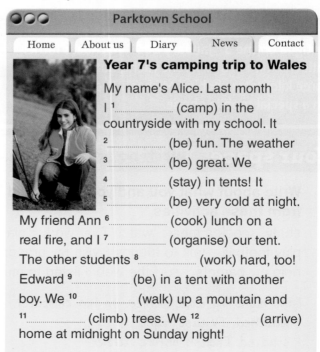

⬤⬤⬤	Parktown School			
Home	About us	Diary	News	Contact

Year 7's camping trip to Wales

My name's Alice. Last month I ¹ _____ (camp) in the countryside with my school. It ² _____ (be) fun. The weather ³ _____ (be) great. We ⁴ _____ (stay) in tents! It ⁵ _____ (be) very cold at night.

My friend Ann ⁶ _____ (cook) lunch on a real fire, and I ⁷ _____ (organise) our tent. The other students ⁸ _____ (work) hard, too! Edward ⁹ _____ (be) in a tent with another boy. We ¹⁰ _____ (walk) up a mountain and ¹¹ _____ (climb) trees. We ¹² _____ (arrive) home at midnight on Sunday night!

5 ◯ **3.28** Listen to Joe and tick (✓) or cross (✗) the boxes.

Last weekend

1 ☐ He listened to music.
2 ☐ He played computer games.
3 ☐ He watched a DVD.
4 ☐ He surfed the web.
5 ☐ He played football.
6 ☐ He played a musical instrument.
7 ☐ He helped his parents in the home.
8 ☐ He visited his grandparents.
9 ☐ He studied for a test.

6 ☆ Work in pairs. Tell your partner about last weekend. Use these verbs.

> stay talk tidy play
> start watch walk work

Last weekend I played football.

7 ✐ Complete the email in the past simple. Use the verbs in Exercise 6.

Hi Lucy
How R U?
On Saturday morning I ¹ _tidied_ my room. In the afternoon I ² _____ tennis in the park with Megan. Then we ³ _____ back to my house. In the evening we ⁴ _____ a DVD and then we ⁵ _____ for hours!
I ⁶ _____ on Sunday morning. Homework! In the afternoon it ⁷ _____ to rain so I ⁸ _____ at home. Tell me about your weekend!
Lots of love
Julia

8 ✐ What did you do last weekend? Write an email. Use the verbs in Exercise 6.

➤ Language check page 142

compound nouns

Some English nouns consist of two words. You know lots already!

football team

packed lunch

text message

computer game

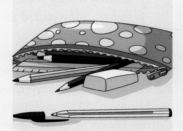

pencil case

orange juice

9 Match the words to make common compound nouns.

1 mobile   a time
2 swimming   b rules
3 phone   c address
4 email   d player
5 free   e number
6 DVD   f centre
7 school   g phone
8 shopping   h pool

10 Write new compound nouns in a special page of your Vocabulary notebook.

Reading and listening

1 **Warm up** **Look at the pictures and the titles and answer the questions.**
Who are the people? What are they doing? What places can you see on the map?

Great travellers

Marco Polo

Marco Polo was a brilliant traveller and storyteller. He was born in Venice, Italy in 1254. When Marco was 17 he started a long journey with his father and uncle. It lasted 24 years! Their journey was difficult because they travelled by horse, camel and ship. They wanted to buy beautiful things. They visited the Middle East, Asia and China. In China, Marco and his family stayed with Kublai Khan's family. Kublai was the leader of China, and he was very rich. He liked Marco and his family – they stayed with him for 17 years. Marco arrived home in 1295, and he never travelled again. In his famous travel book he describes new inventions such as ice cream and paper money!

Ibn Battuta

Ibn Battuta was a great explorer and traveller. He was born in Morocco in 1304. He travelled around the Middle East, India, China and Africa for 30 years!

He lived and worked for nine years in India. He travelled 120,000 kilometres to over 40 countries. His journey was also difficult because he travelled by ship, on foot, and by horse and camel. There weren't any trains, buses or planes! It was very dangerous too – there were terrible storms. We can read about his journey in his wonderful travel book.

2 **3.30** **Read and listen to the article on page 106. Are the sentences true (*T*) or false (*F*)? Correct the false sentences.**

1 Ibn Battuta was born in 1254. F *Marco Polo was born in 1254.*
2 Marco Polo was away from home for 24 years.
3 Marco Polo travelled with his father and brother.
4 Ibn Battuta visited over 40 countries.
5 Both Marco Polo and Ibn Battuta lived in India.
6 Both Ibn Battuta and Marco Polo travelled to China.

3 **Underline the adjectives in the article. What do the adjectives describe?**

4 **Check you understand these words. Use a dictionary or ask your teacher.**

| **Nouns** | astronaut moon parachute step | **Verbs** | orbit land fly parachute step |

5 **3.31** **Listen and match the facts with the person.**
Write *V* (Valentina Tereshkova) or *N* (Neil Armstrong).

first woman to fly in space ☑V☐   returned to Earth on 19 June ☐

born in the USA ☐   first man to walk on the Moon ☐

travelled in the Apollo 11 space ship ☐   born in Russia ☐

travelled in space in 1969 ☐   travelled in the Vostok 6 space ship ☐

returned to Earth on 24 July ☐   travelled in space in 1963 ☐

Neil Armstrong

Speaking

6 **Work in pairs. Match the inventions with the places. Discuss.**
A I think the carpet was a Chinese invention.
B I don't agree. I think the carpet came from the Middle East.
A Really? OK. Let's say China.

Valentina Tereshkova

FACTFILE: INVENTIONS

Many inventions we use every day come from different places.
Where did these things come from? Was it China or the Middle East?

the carpet

the clock

coffee

the toothbrush

chess

paper

the camera

pasta

the umbrella

tea

7 **3.32** **Listen and check.**

Grammar
present continuous as future
• prepositions of time

Functions
talking about the future

Presentation

1 Warm up Look at *Poppy's world* and answer the questions.
Where are Poppy and Jack? What do you think they are doing?
How does Poppy feel in the second picture?

2 ⊙ 3.36 Listen and read the photo story on page 109. Answer the questions.

1 Has Poppy got any plans for the weekend?
2 What is she doing?
3 Where is Poppy going on Saturday morning?
4 Where are they working on Sunday?
5 Has Jack got any plans for Saturday?
6 What time does Jack want to meet Poppy on Saturday morning?

Language focus

• We're **going** to Amy's house on Saturday.
• What **are** you **doing** tomorrow?
• I'm not **playing** football in the morning.

3 Read *Language focus*. Find more examples in *Poppy's world*.

Vocabulary • Weekend activities

4 ⊙ 3.37 Match the activities with the verbs. Then listen and check.

| tennis | my room | at home | a DVD | shopping | a party | home |
| in bed | a picnic | a museum | TV | swimming | computer games | |

play   stay   tidy   go   have   watch   go to

a party

5 Can you add more activities to the spidergrams?

6 Choose activities for Saturday and Sunday. Make notes in the diary.

	Saturday	Sunday
morning		
afternoon		
evening		

7 Work in pairs. Ask and answer questions. Are you doing the same things?
A What are you doing on Saturday morning?
B I'm going to the skate park. What are you doing?
A I'm staying in bed!

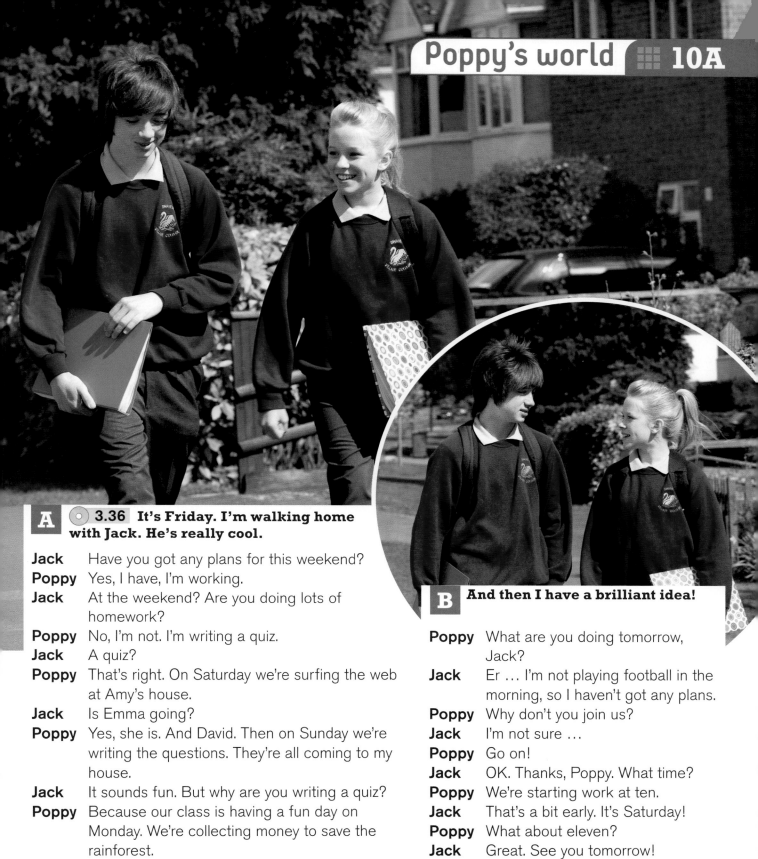

A ⊙ **3.36** **It's Friday. I'm walking home with Jack. He's really cool.**

Jack	Have you got any plans for this weekend?
Poppy	Yes, I have, I'm working.
Jack	At the weekend? Are you doing lots of homework?
Poppy	No, I'm not. I'm writing a quiz.
Jack	A quiz?
Poppy	That's right. On Saturday we're surfing the web at Amy's house.
Jack	Is Emma going?
Poppy	Yes, she is. And David. Then on Sunday we're writing the questions. They're all coming to my house.
Jack	It sounds fun. But why are you writing a quiz?
Poppy	Because our class is having a fun day on Monday. We're collecting money to save the rainforest.

B **And then I have a brilliant idea!**

Poppy	What are you doing tomorrow, Jack?
Jack	Er … I'm not playing football in the morning, so I haven't got any plans.
Poppy	Why don't you join us?
Jack	I'm not sure …
Poppy	Go on!
Jack	OK. Thanks, Poppy. What time?
Poppy	We're starting work at ten.
Jack	That's a bit early. It's Saturday!
Poppy	What about eleven?
Jack	Great. See you tomorrow!

Your space   Describing plans

8 **Write your plans for this weekend.**

On Saturday morning I'm staying at home. I'm visiting my grandparents in the afternoon. On Saturday evening I'm watching TV. On Sunday …

Chat zone

It sounds fun.
I'm not sure.
Go on!

Present continuous for future arrangements

1 **Complete the conversation with short forms if possible.**

Zoe What ..*are*.. you doing on Saturday?
Zak I .... playing chess on Saturday.
Zoe On Sunday?
Zak Oh, my friend Max .... visiting me.
Zoe On Monday evening?
Zak Robopet and I .... going to the park.
Zoe On Tuesday evening?
Zak Erm … sorry!

2 **◉ 3.38 The teacher is telling her students about their day in London. Circle the correct information.**

PARKTOWN SCHOOL

Parktown School visit to London

Saturday

8:30 am	have breakfast / leave the hotel
9:30 am	go on the London Eye / go on a Thames boat trip
11 am	visit the British Museum / visit the Science Museum
1 pm	have a picnic in a park / go to a restaurant
3 pm	go shopping / go sightseeing
7 pm	have dinner / cook dinner
8:30 pm	go to the theatre / go to the cinema
11 pm	go to bed / go to a party

3 **🖉 Imagine you are one of the students. Look at the schedule and answer the questions.**

1 What are you doing at 8:30?
I'm *leaving the hotel at 8:30.*
2 What are you doing at 9:30?
....
3 What time are you visiting a museum?
....
4 Where are you having lunch?
....
5 What are you doing in the afternoon?
....
6 What are you doing at seven o'clock?
....
7 Where are you going after dinner?
....
8 What time are you going to bed?
....

4 **Work in pairs. Ask and answer questions about tomorrow.**

A What are you doing at 11 o'clock?
B I'm having a Maths lesson.

Get it right!

Remember to use the correct tense of the verb:
Tomorrow I'm playing tennis.
NOT ~~Tomorrow I play tennis.~~
Next week I'm visiting my friends.
NOT ~~Next week I visit my friends.~~

Prepositions of time

5 **Complete the tables with these words.**

| dinnertime | March | the evening |
| 8:15 | ~~Wednesday~~ | 17th September |

| on | Monday, Tuesday, Wednesday etc. |
| | 15th May, 21st June, _____ etc. |

in	the morning, the afternoon, _____
	January, February, _____ etc.
	1995, 2008, etc.

| at | midnight, five o'clock, _____ , etc. |
| | night, the weekend, lunchtime, _____ |

| **next** | Thursday, week, weekend, etc. |

| **no preposition** | tomorrow, the day after tomorrow |

6 **Complete the conversations with correct forms of the present continuous.**

1 A: Where _are_ they _meeting_ ? (meet)
  B: At the train station.

2 A: What _____ you _____ on Saturday afternoon? (do)
  B: I' _____ to the shops with my parents. (go)

3 A: _____ he _____ his homework tonight? (do)
  B: Yes, he _____ .

4 A: Anna's mum _____ tomorrow. (not work)
  B: That's right. She' _____ a holiday. (take)

5 A: _____ you _____ the web this evening? (surf)
  B: No, I' _____ .

6 A: What _____ we _____ tonight, Mum? (eat)
  B: Spaghetti.

7 **Work in pairs. Ask and answer questions about your plans for this week.**

A What are you doing on Monday?
B I'm playing football in the school team at five o'clock.

8 **3.39** **Read and complete the conversation. Listen and check.**

Beth: Hi, Larry. Can we check my diary?
Larry: Sure, Beth.
Beth: What ¹ _am I doing_ (I, do) on Friday?
Larry: At nine o'clock ² _____ (you, leave) for the airport, then ³ _____ (you, fly) to LA in the afternoon.
Beth: OK. What ⁴ _____ (I, do) in the evening?
Larry: ⁵ _____ (you, see) Corbin Bleu.
Beth: That's cool. What time ⁶ _____ (I, start) work on Saturday?
Larry: Erm … at eight o'clock.
Beth: That's terrible!
Larry: I'm sorry, but ⁷ _____ (you, do) an interview on AM TV. Then ⁸ _____ (you, meet) Steven Spielberg. ⁹ _____ (you, talk) about a new film.
Beth: What ¹⁰ _____ (happen) in the evening?
Larry: ¹¹ _____ (you, go) to the Oscars.
Beth: ¹² _____ (you, come) with me?
Larry: No, ¹³ _____ (I, stay) in the office.

9 **Work in pairs. Act out the conversation with your partner.**

10B Where is this building?

Presentation

1 **Warm up** **Work with a partner. Answer the questions.**
Do you enjoy doing quizzes? Are you good at them?
Do you like TV quiz programmes?

2 **Work with a partner. Do Poppy's quiz.**
A I think the answer to Number 1 is 'b'.
B I agree.

A I think the answer to Number 2 is 'c'.
B I don't agree. I think it's 'a'.

3 ◉ **3.40** **Listen and check. How many correct answers have you got?**

4 **Work in pairs. Ask the questions.**
Were any of the questions very easy or very difficult?
Were any of the answers surprising?

5 **Work in groups. Write a quiz with six questions.**

Language focus

Revision
- What **is** this Roman number?
- A football team **has got** …
- Which of these animals **lives** in a rainforest?
- They**'re skiing**.
- A goldfish **can** remember things …
- You **must** not send text messages.
- Julius Caesar **was** … .
- … **painted** this painting.

OUR FANTASTIC QUIZ

Try our quiz for 50p! And help save the rainforests.

Get 18 correct answers and win a prize.
Quiz by Poppy, Amy, Emma, David and Jack

1 Which of these animals lives in a rainforest?
a kangaroo
b monkey
c lion

2 Who painted this picture?
a Leonardo da Vinci
b Pablo Picasso
c Vincent Van Gogh

3 Dinosaurs lived on Earth for about …
a 10 million years
b 150 million years
c 15 thousand years

4 What does www mean on the internet?
 a world wonder web
 b world wide web
 c wide world web

5 Which country has this flag?
 a the USA
 b Japan
 c the UK

6 This person is writing 'My name is' in ...
 a Chinese
 b Russian
 c Greek

7 This sign means you must not ...
 a send text messages
 b carry a mobile phone
 c use your mobile phone

8 What is this Roman number?
 a four
 b five
 c six

VI

9 Where can you see these boats?
 a London
 b Paris
 c Egypt

10 What is he doing?
 a He's skiing.
 b He's riding.
 c He's juggling.

11 Where is this building?
 a China
 b the USA
 c Mexico

12 Elephants drink about ... of water a day.
 a 2 litres
 b 500 litres
 c 90 litres

13 Tutankhamun was an ...
 a ancient Greek
 b ancient Egyptian
 c ancient Roman

14 A goldfish can remember things for ...
 a 3 seconds
 b 3 days
 c 3 months

15 What English city was the pop group The Beatles from?
 a Manchester
 b Cambridge
 c Liverpool

16 A football team has got ...
 a 12 players
 b 11 players
 c 15 players

17 Most people in Brazil speak ...
 a Spanish
 b Portuguese
 c English

18 ... is the author of the Harry Potter novels.
 a J.R.R. Tolkien
 b J.K. Rowling
 c J.M. Barrie

Talking about possessions

1 Complete the questions. Then (circle) the answer for you.

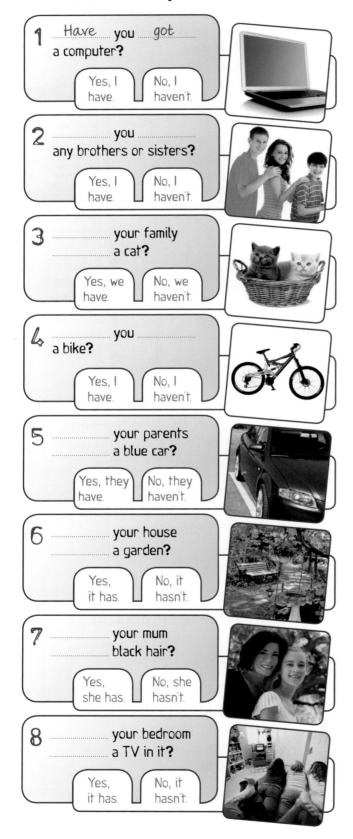

1 Have you got a computer?
  Yes, I have. | No, I haven't.

2 .... you .... any brothers or sisters?
  Yes, I have. | No, I haven't.

3 .... your family .... a cat?
  Yes, we have. | No, we haven't.

4 .... you .... a bike?
  Yes, I have. | No, I haven't.

5 .... your parents .... a blue car?
  Yes, they have. | No, they haven't.

6 .... your house .... a garden?
  Yes, it has. | No, it hasn't.

7 .... your mum .... black hair?
  Yes, she has. | No, she hasn't.

8 .... your bedroom .... a TV in it?
  Yes, it has. | No, it hasn't.

2 ⚑ Work in pairs. Ask and answer the questions. Remember your partner's answers.

3 ✎ Write sentences about your partner.

Talking about the present

4 📖 Read and complete the email with the present continuous or the present simple.

○○○

Hi Milly
I'**1** m writing (write) this email after dinner and I'**2** .... (listen) to music.
Let me tell you about me and my life. I'm twelve and I **3** .... (live) in Leeds.
I **4** .... (go) to a new school and I've got lots of new friends. Laura and Ann **5** .... (live) near me. They are sisters, but they're very different. Laura **6** .... (like) Maths, but Ann **7** .... (like) Art!
At the moment my mum and dad **8** .... (watch) TV and my big brother Tim **9** .... (do) homework in his room.
Oh, my mum'**10** .... (call) me. It's time for bed. I must go.
Write soon and tell me about your life.
Jane

5 Write questions and answers about you.
  1 Where do you live ? (live)
    I live in Mexico City.
  2 What .... you .... at the moment? (do)
  3 What football team .... you .... ? (like)
  4 How .... you .... to school? (get)
  5 What time .... you .... in the morning? (get up)
  6 What .... your best friend .... at the moment? (do)

6 ⚑ Work in pairs. Ask your partner the questions.

Talking about skills and abilities

7 🔘 **3.41** Complete the table.

	play computer games	play the guitar	play football	play tennis	make films	swim
Fred	no	yes	no	yes	no	no
Erin	yes	no	no	yes	no	yes
Molly						
Lucas						
Tilly						

8 **Complete the sentences about the friends. Use *can* or *can't*.**

1 Lucas ..can play.. football.
2 Fred .... computer games.
3 Tilly .... football.
4 Molly and Lucas .... make films.
5 Fred and Molly .... swim.
6 Erin .... the guitar, but she .... play tennis.
7 Fred .... films, but he .... the guitar.
8 Erin, Lucas and Tilly .... swim.

9 🗨 **Work in pairs. Tell your partner about you.**

A I can play computer games.
B Me too.

➡ **Language check page 142**

because

- Use *because* to give a reason.

*I like my gran **because** she's kind.*

- Use *because* to answer a **Why** question.

***Why** have you got all these scary DVDs?*
***Because** I love horror films.*

- Use *because* to join two ideas.

*Adam is in the dark **because** the light doesn't work.*

then

- Use (*and*) *then* to talk about the next thing.
  *Turn on the TV and **then** press this button.*

- **You can begin a sentence with *then*.**
  *We visited the museum. **Then** we had lunch.*

10 **Complete the sentences with *because* or *then*.**

1 First open your books at page 18, ... look at the picture.
2 This computer is no good .... it is old.
3 Emma is having special lessons .... she is bad at Maths.
4 He has breakfast and .... he walks to work.
5 I can't go to the cinema with you .... I've got a cold.

Reading

1 **Warm up Look at the photos. What can you see?**

a big ape [3]   a sea monster [ ]   an ancient city [ ]   a space ship [ ]

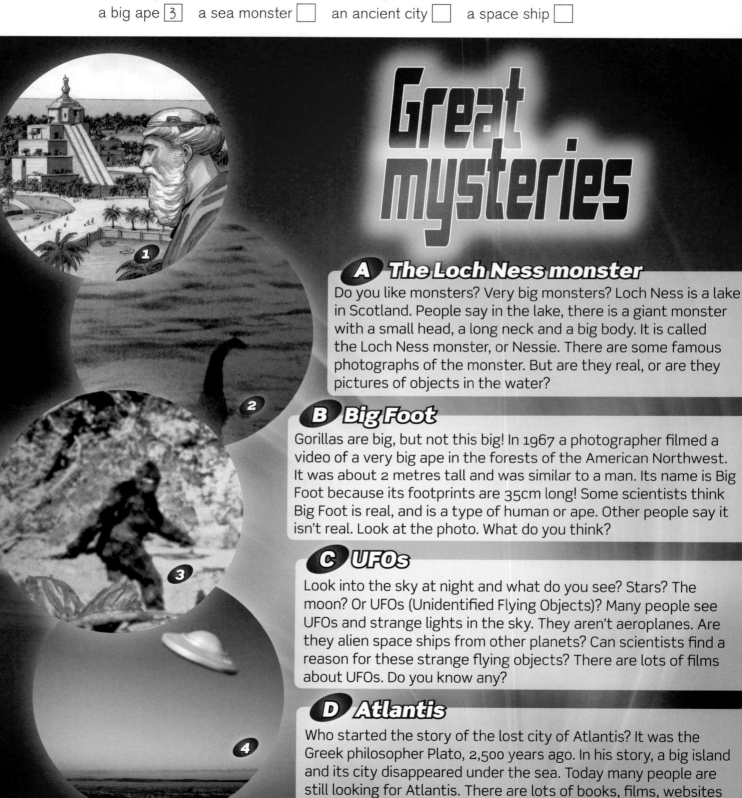

Great mysteries

A The Loch Ness monster

Do you like monsters? Very big monsters? Loch Ness is a lake in Scotland. People say in the lake, there is a giant monster with a small head, a long neck and a big body. It is called the Loch Ness monster, or Nessie. There are some famous photographs of the monster. But are they real, or are they pictures of objects in the water?

B Big Foot

Gorillas are big, but not this big! In 1967 a photographer filmed a video of a very big ape in the forests of the American Northwest. It was about 2 metres tall and was similar to a man. Its name is Big Foot because its footprints are 35cm long! Some scientists think Big Foot is real, and is a type of human or ape. Other people say it isn't real. Look at the photo. What do you think?

C UFOs

Look into the sky at night and what do you see? Stars? The moon? Or UFOs (Unidentified Flying Objects)? Many people see UFOs and strange lights in the sky. They aren't aeroplanes. Are they alien space ships from other planets? Can scientists find a reason for these strange flying objects? There are lots of films about UFOs. Do you know any?

D Atlantis

Who started the story of the lost city of Atlantis? It was the Greek philosopher Plato, 2,500 years ago. In his story, a big island and its city disappeared under the sea. Today many people are still looking for Atlantis. There are lots of books, films, websites and cartoons about the mystery. Is it under the Atlantic Ocean? Is it in the Mediterranean? What do you think? Was there really an island called Atlantis? Or was it just Plato's story?

2 Read the article on page 116 quickly and match the paragraphs with the photos.

A ☐　　B ☐　　C ☐　　D ☐

3 Read the article again and write the mysteries.

1 A city disappeared under the sea.　*Atlantis*

2 Strange objects fly in the sky.

3 A large animal lives in a lake.

4 A big ape lives in a forest.

Listening

4 Look at the pictures below. What is happening in each one?

5 ◉ **3.43** Listen to the people phoning their friends and write the numbers 1-4..

6 Work in pairs. Say what you believe in / don't believe in.

I don't believe in the Loch Ness monster.

I think I believe in Atlantis.

Speaking

7 Work in pairs. Talk about some of the topics below.

Writing

8 Choose a topic from Exercise 7 and write a paragraph about it.

Greetings, introductions and saying goodbye

1 Warm up Look at the pictures and answer the questions.

Is it a special day? Why?

A

Katie	Hello! Come in.
Nick	Happy birthday, Katie.
Katie	Thanks!
Nick	Hello, Mrs King.
Mrs King	Hello, Nick. How are you?
Nick	Fine, thanks. And you?
Mrs King	I'm OK, thanks.

B

Katie	Nick, this is my friend, Samira.
Nick	Hi, Samira.
Samira	Hello, Nick. Nice to meet you.

C

Samira	Hi! I'm Samira.
Ruby	Hi! My name's Ruby. Where are you from, Samira?
Samira	I'm from India. I'm here on holiday.

D

Nick	Bye. Thanks for a great party.
Mrs King	Goodbye, Nick.

2 🔘 **1.38 Read and listen to the conversations. (Circle) the correct answer.**

1	It's	**a** Katie's birthday	**b** Nick's birthday
2	Samira is	**a** Katie's friend	**b** Katie's sister
3	Samira is from	**a** Ireland	**b** India

3 🔘 **1.39 Look at *Phrasebook*. Listen and complete the conversation.**

4 In groups of three, practise the conversation in *Phrasebook*.

Phrasebook

Emily Hi, Sam. How
¹ .... you?

Sam I'm fine, thanks.

Emily This is ² ....
friend, Lucy.

Sam Hi, Lucy. ³ ....
Sam.

Lucy ⁴ ...., Sam.
Nice to meet
⁵ ....

Asking for and giving personal information

Robert	Hi. Can I join the Sports Club, please?
Lucy	Of course. What's your first name?
Robert	Robert.
Lucy	And what's your family name?
Robert	Stevenson.
Lucy	Can you spell that, please?
Robert	S-T-E-V-E-N-S-O-N.
Lucy	What's your address?
Robert	Erm … 12 New Street, Oxford, OX6 8TB.
Lucy	Sorry, can you repeat that, please?
Robert	12 New Street, Oxford, OX6 8TB.
Lucy	What's your phone number?
Robert	01967 554282.
Lucy	Thanks. What's your nationality?
Robert	I'm British.
Lucy	And how old are you?
Robert	Twelve.
Lucy	OK, that's fine.

1 **Warm up Look at the picture and answer the questions.**

Where is Robert? Where is he from? How old is he?

2 ⊙ **1.52** **Read and listen to the conversation. Check your answers to Exercise 1.**

3 ⊙ **1.52** **Listen again and complete the form.**

> ⊙ **ROSE HILL SPORTS CLUB** *New member*
>
> *First name:* ....
> *Family name:* ....
> *Address:* ....
> ....
> *Phone number:* ....
> *Nationality:* ....
> *Age:* ....

4 **Work in pairs. Practise the conversation.**

5 ⊙ **1.53** **Look at *Phrasebook*. Listen and complete the sentences.**

6 **Copy the form in Exercise 3. Complete it for your partner.**

> **Phrasebook**
>
> Can you ¹............... that, please?
> Sorry, can you ²............... that, please?
> Yes, that's ³................. .

Exchanging email addresses

1 ⊙ **2.13** **Listen and repeat.**

1 • (dot) **2** @ (at) **3** — (hyphen) **4** co **5** net **6** com

2 ⊙ **2.14** **Work in pairs. Read the email addresses. Then listen and check.**

1 jenny.pearce@yellow.net **3** fox-david@appletree.co.uk
2 littleduck@nbdkpp.com **4** zoe3@helloworld.net

3 Warm up **Look at the picture and describe the children.**

4 ⊙ **2.15** **Listen to the conversation and write Tim's email address.**

Tim's email: ....

5 ⊙ **2.15** **Listen again and repeat the conversation.**

Lan	Hi, Tim.
Tim	Hi, Lan.
Lan	I've got a good photo for our school project. Look!
Tim	Wow, it's great!
Lan	I've got the photo on our computer at home.
Tim	Can you email it to me?
Lan	Sure. What's your email address?
Tim	It's ....
Lan	Is that one word?
Tim	Yes, it is.
Lan	OK.
Tim	Cool. Thanks, Lan!

6 ⊙ **2.16** **Look at** *Phrasebook*. **Listen and complete the sentences.**

7 **Invent an email address. Work in pairs. Practise the conversation.**

A Can you send me an email?
B Sure. What's your email address?

Phrasebook

Can you ¹ .... it to me?
What's ² .... email address?
Is that ³ .... word?

Buying a ticket

1 Warm up **Look at the poster and answer the questions.**

When is Beppo's Circus in Cambridge? How do you buy tickets?

2 ◉ **2.28** **Read and listen to the conversation. Circle the correct word.**

BEPPO'S CIRCUS

Midsummer Common, Cambridge, 15th to 18th March

Come and see the best clowns, acrobats, trapeze artists and circus horses

"A fantastic show"

For tickets, go to the tent at Midsummer Common or call: 0521 431894

Woman	Hello, can I help you?
George	Yes, please. What time does the show start?
Woman	It starts at ¹ (**6 o'clock**) / **7 o'clock**.
George	How much are the tickets?
Woman	Well, for children up to 16 years it's ² **£3 / £5** and for adults it's ³ **£7 / £9**.
George	Oh, that's good. I'm ⁴ **12 / 13** and my brother's ⁵ **14 / 15**. I'd like four tickets, please – two adults and two children.
Woman	That's ⁶ **£24 / £28**, please.
George	Here you are.
Woman	Here are your tickets and your change.

3 ◉ **2.28** **Listen and repeat the conversation.**

4 ◉ **2.29** **Look at *Phrasebook*. Listen and complete the sentences.**

5 **Work in pairs. Practise the conversations with different information.**

A Hello. Can I help you?
B Yes, please. What time does the show start?
A It starts at 8 o'clock.

Phrasebook

Can I ¹............... you?
What time does the show ²...............?
How much are the ³...............?
I'd like four tickets, ⁴...............
⁵............... £28, please.
Here you ⁶...............
⁷............... are your tickets and your change.

Making suggestions

1 ⊙ **2.39** **Listen and complete the conversations.**

Peter Let's ¹_____ swimming.
Dan I can't swim. Let's ²_____ to the park and ride our ³_____ .
Peter That's a ⁴_____ idea.

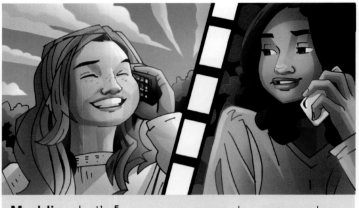

Maddie Let's ⁵_____ computer games at my house.
Isabel I'm sorry, I can't ⁶_____ this evening. I've got a piano lesson.
Maddie No problem. ⁷_____ meet tomorrow.
Isabel Yes, that's a good idea.

2 ⊙ **2.40** **Look at** *Phrasebook*. **Listen and complete the conversations.**

3 **Work in pairs. Practise the conversations in Exercise 1 with different activities.**

4 **Read the emails and answer the questions.**

1 What does Ryan suggest?
2 What does Josh answer?
3 What does Josh suggest?

Phrasebook

1
A Let's ¹_____ TV.
B I'm sorry, I ²_____ . I'm tired.
A No problem.
2
A Let's ³_____ swimming.
B That's a good idea. Let's ⁴_____ later.

To: Josh
From: Ryan
Subject: Football

Hi Josh

Are you free tomorrow afternoon? Let's play football with Archie and Connor.

Ryan

To: Ryan
From: Josh
Subject: Football

Hi Ryan

That's a good idea. Let's have an ice cream, too.

Josh

5 **Write an email to your partner. Suggest that you do something together. Then answer your partner's email.**

Invitations

1 Warm up **Answer the questions.**

What do you usually do on your birthday? Do you like parties?

2 ⊙ **2.55 Listen and complete the conversation. Then practise it with your partner.**

Alex	Hi, Jessica.
Jessica	Hi, Alex.
Alex	Would you like to come to a ¹............................ ?
Jessica	A party?
Alex	Yes, it's my ²............................ party. Would you like to come?
Jessica	Yes, I would. When is it?
Alex	It's on Saturday at ³............................ o'clock. At Mario's pizza restaurant.
Jessica	Brilliant. See you on ⁴............................ .
Alex	Great.

3 ⊙ **2.56 Listen and put the invitations in order. Which invitation does Jessica accept?**

play tennis with Kathy ☐   see a film with Liam ☐
play a computer game with Alice ☐

4 ⊙ **2.57 Look at *Phrasebook*. Listen and repeat.**

5 **Work in pairs. Practise the conversations.**

6 **Read the invitation and answer the questions.**

1 Whose birthday is it?   **2** Where is the party?
3 What day and time is it?

Phrasebook

making an invitation
Would you like to come to a party?
accepting an invitation
Yes, I would.
Sure. / OK.
refusing an invitation
I'm sorry, I can't. I've got a piano lesson.

It's my 13th birthday!   *Let's go bowling!*

Name Owen Jones
Date Saturday 18th June
Time 12 o'clock
Location Cambridge Leisure Park, Clifton Way, Cambridge
Email owen3jones@brit.com

7 **Write a party invitation and give it to your partner. Accept or refuse your partner's invitation.**

Dear (*name*),
Thank you for your invitation.
I would like to … / I'm sorry, I can't … (*add an excuse*).
See you on …
(*name*)

Ordering food

1 **◎ 3.09** What do Ethan and Jade order? Listen and write *E* (Ethan) or *J* (Jade) on the menu. Then complete the conversation.

Today's menu

Main meals

Vegetable lasagne
Fish and chips
Chicken curry
Jacket potatoes:
– cheese
– tuna and mayonnaise
Mixed salad

Desserts

Apple pie
Yoghurt
Fruit (an apple,
a banana or an orange)
Ice cream

Drinks

Mineral water
Apple/Orange juice
Milk

School cook	Hello. What would you like?
Ethan	Can I have ¹........, please?
School cook	Anything else?
Ethan	I'd like some ²........, please.
School cook	Here you are.
Ethan	Thanks.
School cook	Hello. What would you like?
Jade	Have you got any ³........?
School cook	Yes, we've got ⁴........ .

Jade	Mmm. Can I have ⁵........, please?
School cook	Yes, of course. Would you like a dessert?
Jade	Yes, can I have ⁶........?
School cook	Here you are.
Jade	Thank you.

2 **◎ 3.09** Listen again and repeat the conversation.

3 **◎ 3.10** Look at *Phrasebook*. Listen and number the sentences.

4 In groups practise new conversations like the one in Exercise 1. Change the food that you order.

Phrasebook

School cook

What would you like? [1]

Would you like a dessert? [ ]

Here you are. [ ]

Anything else? [ ]

Student

Can I have a jacket potato with cheese, please? [ ]

I'd like an apple, please. [ ]

Yes, please. / No, thanks. / Thank you. [ ]

Asking the way and giving directions

1 **Warm up** **Which building is ...**

1 opposite the post office? ....

2 next to the cinema? ....

3 opposite the supermarket? ....

4 next to the sports centre? ....

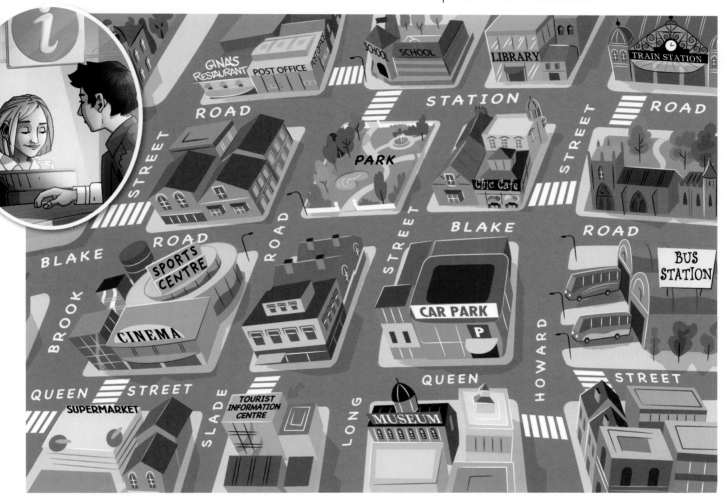

2 🔊 **3.19** **You are at the Tourist Information Centre. Match the questions with the directions, then listen and check.**

1 Excuse me, where's the bus station?

2 Excuse me, where's the library?

3 Excuse me, where's the sports centre?

a Go left. Then turn right. It's on the left in Slade Road. It's next to the cinema.

b Go right. Take the first left. Go straight on. It's on the right.

c Go right. Go straight on. Take the second left. It's on the right in Howard Street.

3 🔊 **3.20** **Look at *Phrasebook*. Listen and repeat.**

4 **Work in pairs. Practise asking and giving directions.**

Phrasebook

1 Excuse me, where's the train station?

2 Go left. Take the first left. Go straight on. Take the second right. Take the first left. It's on the right.

3 Thank you very much.

4 You're welcome.

9 Communication

Buying train and bus tickets

1 🔘 **3.33** Read and complete the conversation. Then listen and check.

> Are you under 16?
> Platform 4. The next train is at 10:45.
> That's £5.60 each.
> Single or return?

DEPARTURES	
DESTINATION	TIME
BIRMINGHAM	10:10
MANCHESTER	10:37
LONDON	10:45
BRISTOL	11:05
OXFORD	11:28
BOURNEMOUTH	11:45

Becky   Can I have two tickets to London, please?

Man   ¹...

Becky   Return, please.

Man   ²...

James   Yes, we're 12.

Man   ³...

James   What platform does the next train leave from?

Man   ⁴...

James   Thank you.

2 🔘 **3.34** Read and complete the conversation. Then listen and check.

> tickets   2.50   Here   change   thank you

James   Two ¹.................. to the city centre, please.

Bus driver   Child fare?

James   Yes, please.

Bus driver   £ ².................. , please.

Becky   ³.................. you are.

Bus driver   Thanks. Take your ⁴.................. !

James   Oh, ⁵.................. .

3 Work in a group of three. Act out the conversations.

4 🔘 **3.35** Look at *Phrasebook*. Listen and complete.

Phrasebook

Can I have two
¹.................. to London,
please?
Single or return?
Single, please.
².................. , please.

On a train

What ³.................. does
the next train leave
from?

10 Communication

Making and suggesting plans

1 🔘 **3.44** The students are making plans for next week. Number the two conversations in the correct order. Then listen and check.

1 **Daniel** That sounds great. ☐
Jack Why don't we listen to music? ☐
Daniel No, I'm not. ☐
Jack Are you doing anything on Monday morning? ☐1☐

2 **Emily** That's a pity. Are you free on Wednesday morning? ☐
Emily Fantastic! ☐
Emily Let's go to a museum on Tuesday afternoon. ☐
Yasmin I'm sorry. I'm playing tennis with Jo. ☐
Yasmin Yes, I am. ☐

2 🔘 **3.45** Listen and complete *Phrasebook*. Then listen again and repeat.

3 Write two appointments in your diary for next week, e.g. *go to the dentist* or *visit my grandparents*. You can choose the day and time.

Phrasebook

Why ¹.............. we play tennis on Tuesday afternoon?
² .... go to the cinema on Thursday afternoon.
That sounds ³.............. .
Good ⁴.............. !
I'm ⁵.............. .
I'm visiting my grandparents.
That's a pity.

	Monday	Tuesday	Wednesday	Thursday	Friday
morning					
afternoon					

4 Think of two interesting activities to do with your classmates next week, e.g. *go to the cinema*. Write them in the diary too.

5 Work in groups. Invite your classmates to do activities with you. Write the names of the students who say 'yes'. Use *Phrasebook* to help you.

The Mystery Game

by Martyn Hobbs

Contents

The BLACK CAT

Episode 1 ○ 3.46

1. IT'S A COLD SUNDAY AFTERNOON IN NOVEMBER. DAISY IS IN THE MUSEUM WITH HER PARENTS AND HER FRIEND NATHAN.

LOOK! A CHINESE VASE!

IT'S VERY OLD.

3. BUT NATHAN ISN'T BORED - HISTORY IS HIS FAVOURITE SUBJECT.

THIS VASE IS FROM GREECE.

IT'S BEAUTIFUL. AND IT'S VERY OLD, TOO.

2. DAISY IS BORED.

HMMM.

4. HEY, LISTEN!

WHAT IS IT?

I DON'T KNOW.

MEOW!

BUT IT'S OVER HERE.

LET'S GO!

5. IT'S A CAT!

MEOW!

A CAT IN A MUSEUM? THAT'S STRANGE! WHERE IS IT?

THERE! IT'S IN THE ROOM!

6. A CAT IS NEAR THE DOOR. IT'S SMALL AND BLACK AND VERY PRETTY.

COME ON!

Episode 2 ◉ 3.47

The MAP and the DICE

1
DAISY AND NATHAN ARE OUTSIDE THE ROOM WITH THE VASES.

WHERE'S THE CAT?

THERE IT IS!

2
AT THE END OF THE CORRIDOR IS A GREEN DOOR. AND NEXT TO THE DOOR IS THE BLACK CAT.

LET'S GO!

3
THE ROOM BEHIND THE GREEN DOOR IS VERY SMALL. THERE IS AN OLD BICYCLE, AN OLD DESK, SIX UMBRELLAS AND LOTS OF OLD BOXES.

WOW! THIS IS A MESS.

BEEP! BEEP!

WHAT IS IT?

IT'S A TEXT MESSAGE.

4
Open the black box

WHO'S THE MESSAGE FROM?

I DON'T KNOW.

IT'S UNDER THE CAT!

WHERE'S THE BLACK BOX?

5
INSIDE THE BOX THERE IS A MAP AND A DICE.

IT'S JUST AN OLD GAME.

HEY, LOOK AT THIS!

NO, IT ISN'T. THIS ISN'T A NORMAL DICE. THERE ARE TWELVE NUMBERS ON IT. AND LOOK AT THIS MAP! THERE ARE LOTS OF PLACES WITH NUMBERS ON THEM. AMERICA, ITALY, BRAZIL...

6
WHOOSH!

NATHAN... WHAT'S THAT STRANGE LIGHT? AND WHAT'S THAT NOISE?

Episode 3 3.48
Where are we?

Episode 4 ○ 3.49

Roll the Dice!

THEY WALK TO THE CENTRE OF SYDNEY. AFTER HALF AN HOUR THEY SEE AN AMAZING BRIDGE.

WOW! IT'S BEAUTIFUL.

THERE'S A MESSAGE ON YOUR MOBILE.

You have got the Mystery Game! Now roll the dice!

DAISY IS EXCITED BUT NATHAN IS SERIOUS.

WHAT DO YOU THINK, NATHAN? DO WE ROLL THE DICE?

DAISY AND NATHAN TALK ABOUT TRICKY.

TRICKY LIVES IN RIVER ROAD... BUT WHERE'S RIVER ROAD?

ERM, LET'S GO IN THAT DIRECTION. OK TRICKY, FOLLOW ME!

MEON?

1

2

3

WE'VE GOT A PROBLEM. I'VE GOT THE MAP. BUT WHERE'S THE DICE?

4

THEY SEE A TALL MAN WITH LONG, DARK HAIR AND A BEARD. AND HE'S GOT THE DICE!

HEY, WHAT'S THIS? IT'S A DICE... BUT IT'S GOT 12 NUMBERS!

YES, I KNOW. IT'S MINE.

WELL, I LIKE IT. I THINK IT'S MINE.

WHAT DO WE DO?

5

DAISY ROLLS THE DICE. THEY SEE A STRANGE LIGHT AND HEAR A STRANGE NOISE...

8

BUT TRICKY HAS GOT AN IDEA. SHE JUMPS...

HEY!

MEON?

...AND SHE TAKES THE DICE TO DAISY.

6

7

QUICK, DAISY! ROLL THE DICE!

WHOOSH!

Episode 5 ⦿ 3.50

In the JUNGLE

DAISY, NATHAN AND TRICKY CAN'T SEE A CITY NOW. THEY CAN SEE TREES... LOTS OF TREES, AND A BIG RED AND GREEN PARROT!

WOW! THIS IS FANTASTIC! I LOVE TRAVELLING TO THESE DIFFERENT PLACES. WHERE ARE WE NOW?

WELL, WE'RE IN A JUNGLE. IN INDIA? OR AFRICA?

1 I DON'T KNOW. BUT TRICKY DOESN'T LIKE THE INSECTS!

MEOW!

2

3 IT'S ANOTHER TEXT MESSAGE. IT SAYS, 'CAN YOU SEE CROCODILES?'

CROCODILES? WHY CROCODILES? THAT'S...

THEY WALK THROUGH THE JUNGLE. THEY DON'T SEE CROCODILES, BUT DAISY SEES...

LOOK! THERE'S A BEAUTIFUL BLACK GORILLA UNDER THAT TREE.

IT'S SCARY.

SSHH. I CAN HEAR A NOISE.

4 DON'T BE SILLY. GORILLAS ARE SHY ANIMALS. THEY ONLY EAT PLANTS AND FRUIT...

THEY SEE TWO MEN. AND THE MEN HAVE GOT GUNS!

5 THAT POOR GORILLA. WHAT CAN WE DO?

SIT DOWN, DAISY!

DON'T SHOOT THAT GORILLA!

HEY! WHO ARE YOU?

COME HERE!

6 THE MEN ARE ANGRY... BUT THE GORILLA CLIMBS UP INTO THE TREE. IT'S SAFE!

ROLL THE DICE, NATHAN!

SO NATHAN ROLLS THE DICE AND THEY SEE THE STRANGE LIGHT...

WHOOSH!

7

Episode 6 ● 3.51

The Wide Blue Sea

Episode 7 · 3.52

Where's Tricky?

DAISY, NATHAN AND TRICKY ARE NEXT TO A RIVER. THERE ARE TALL TREES ON BOTH SIDES OF THE WATER. BEAUTIFUL PINK BIRDS FLY IN THE SKY.

THEY'RE FLAMINGOS!

WHERE DO FLAMINGOS COME FROM?

SO WE DON'T KNOW WHERE WE ARE.

ERM... AFRICA, SOUTH AMERICA, THE UNITED STATES...

1

DAISY IS TIRED AND HUNGRY.

IS THERE ANYTHING TO EAT?

THERE ISN'T MUCH. I'VE GOT TWO SWEETS. HERE, HAVE ONE.

THANKS.

2

THEY CAN'T SEE THE LITTLE BLACK CAT.

WHERE'S TRICKY? WE CAN'T FIND HER IN THIS JUNGLE.

I WANT TO GO HOME.

ME TOO. LET'S ROLL THE DICE.

3

SO WE'RE IN AMERICA.

I'VE GOT A TEXT MESSAGE. IT SAYS 'WELCOME TO FLORIDA!'

AND IT ALSO SAYS 'LOOK AND LISTEN!'

THEY HEAR AN ENGINE, THEN THEY SEE A WOMAN IN JEANS AND A T-SHIRT ON A BOAT. NEXT TO HER SITS A LITTLE BLACK CAT. TRICKY!

MEOW!

5

NATHAN PICKS UP THE DICE AND DAISY LOOKS AT THE GREEN WATER. AND SHE SEES TWO EYES!

NATHAN! DON'T THROW THE DICE!

WHY NOT?

LOOK AT THE WATER! IT'S A CROCODILE!

4

6

Episode 8 ○ 3.53

Home Again

Unit 1

1 **Circle** the correct words.

1 _____ is my best friend, Tom.
  a (He) **b** She **c** We

2 _____ are from Ireland.
  a I **b** He **c** They

3 _____ is my little sister, Abigail.
  a She **b** He **c** We

4 _____ is my brother, Oliver.
  a His **b** He's **c** He

5 They _____ from New York.
  a are **b** is **c** am

6 Is your name Mario?
  a No, it isn't. **b** No, he isn't.
  c Yes, he is.

7 Is Valentino Rossi Spanish?
  a No, it isn't. **b** No, he isn't.
  c No, she isn't.

8 My cat _____ black, it's white.
  a is **b** aren't **c** isn't

9 I _____ at school. I'm at home.
  a not **b** aren't **c** 'm not

10 Are you hungry?
  a Yes, I is. **b** Yes, I am. **c** Yes, I are.

2 **Write the sentences with the correct personal pronoun.**

1 <u>Tom</u> is my friend. *He is my friend.*

2 <u>The guitar</u> is in my room.

3 <u>My mum and dad</u> are from Ireland.

4 <u>My sister</u> is five.

5 <u>Tom and I</u> are Real Madrid fans.

6 <u>Ben</u> is sixteen.

3 ◎ **1.35** **Listen and complete the text.**

Hi, my name' **¹** _s_____ Adam and
I' **²** _____ from London. My best friend
³ _____ Michael. My favourite football
team **⁴** _____ Manchester United. But
his favourite team **⁵** _____ Manchester
United. It's Chelsea! We' **⁶** _____ twelve
years old. Our interests **⁷** _____ computer
games and music. My parents **⁸** _____
British. Michael is from Britain, but his parents
⁹ _____ . They' **¹⁰** _____ from
Greece.

Unit 2

1 **Complete the email with *I'm, he's, she's, is* or *are*.**

Hi! My name's Jamie. **¹** I'm_____ from
Sydney in Australia. My brother, George,
is fourteen. **²** _____ good fun. My
sister, Lily, **³** _____ eight. My parents
⁴ _____ teachers. My favourite actor is
Jessica Alba. **⁵** _____ very beautiful.
Bye for now,
Jamie

2 **Look at the text and complete the sentences with *there's, there isn't* or *there are*.**

> **Holiday house in sunny Cornwall**
> Attractive house five minutes from the beach
> large living room   two bathrooms
> new kitchen   small garden
> three bedrooms

1 There's_____ a living room.

2 _____ a new kitchen.

3 _____ a dining room.

4 _____ two bathrooms.

5 _____ a big garden.

6 _____ three bedrooms.

3 ◎ **1.50** **Listen and complete the text.**

I'm Iona. **¹** My_____ brother is Piotr.
² _____ names are Polish. **³** _____
parents are from Poland. **⁴** _____ home
town is Krakow. We live **⁵** _____ Dublin.
⁶ _____ house is in the centre of town,
⁷ _____ of a park. **⁸** _____ favourite
room is my bedroom. The walls are red. There
are lots of cushions **⁹** _____ my bed
and a big rug **¹⁰** _____ it. There's an old
armchair **¹¹** _____ of the window and a
lamp on a table **¹²** _____ it.

Unit 3

1 Rewrite the sentences with the possessive 's.

1 This is her favourite film. (Molly)
This is Molly's favourite film.

2 Their parents are from Paris. (Nathan and Lucy)

3 His name is Billy. (My dog)

4 Her mother is forty-five. (Ellie)

5 Their home is in London. (My grandparents)

6 Their lessons are in this classroom. (The students)

7 Where are his books? (Daniele)

8 That is their car. (my uncle and aunt)

2 Circle the correct words.

1 .... you got a pen pal?
a Has **b** Have **c** Is

2 .... pen is that?
a Where **b** How **c** Whose

3 Is this mobile phone .... ?
a yours **b** you **c** your

4 I .... got a skateboard.
a hasn't **b** haven't **c** am

5 Have they got a car? No, they ....
a haven't **b** hasn't **c** isn't

6 That exercise book isn't ....
a my **b** mine **c** me

7 They've .... a house in Spain.
a are **b** have **c** got

8 .... you got lots of cousins?
a Have **b** Has **c** Got

9 Mr Sinclair isn't your teacher. He's ....
a ours **b** our **c** we

10 .... is the girl in the photo?
a Whose **b** Who **c** How

3 ◉ **2.10 Listen and complete the text.**

My name's Daisy and I'm from Cardiff.
[1] *I've* .... got a big family. I've [2] ....
two brothers and a sister. My [3] ....
names are James and Andrew. My [4] ....
name is Olivia. James is ten and Andrew is
sixteen. [5] .... got lots of computer
games. Olivia [6] .... only seven. She's
very shy. [7] .... got a bike! [8] ....
got lots of aunts and uncles. Auntie Lydia is my
favourite. [9] .... funny. Her husband is
my Uncle Rob. [10] .... very clever.

Unit 4

1 Circle the correct form of the verb.

1 Ella **walks / walk** to school with her friends.

2 I **has / have** toast and jam for breakfast.

3 They **has / have** football practice on Thursday.

4 School **starts / start** at half past eight.

5 We **watches / watch** TV in the evening.

6 I **goes / go** to sleep at about ten o'clock.

7 My sister **plays / play** football in the school team.

8 She **has / have** lunch at her grandparents' house.

2 Circle the correct words.

1 Ben .... computer games.
a doesn't play **b** don't play **c** not plays

2 We .... this shop.
a doesn't like **b** don't like **c** don't likes

3 They .... the web in the morning.
a don't surf **b** surf not **c** not surf

4 .... Chiara write a blog?
a Do **b** Don't **c** Does

5 .... do your parents do in their free time?
a What **b** Where **c** When

6 Do you like pizzas?
a Yes, I like. **b** Yes, I do. **c** Yes, I do like.

7 Sophie .... her mum.
a helps **b** help **c** she help

8 .... a shower in the morning?
a Does you have **b** Have you got
c Do you have

3 ◉ **2.24 Listen and complete the text with one or two words in each gap.**

I [1] *get up* .... at half past six. I [2] ....
washed and get dressed. I [3] ....
with my family. We [4] .... cereal,
milk and fruit. School [5] .... at half
past eight and [6] .... at half past
three. I [7] .... at school. My friend
and I [8] .... home. I [9] .... my
homework and then I [10] .... computer
games. We [11] .... dinner at half past
six. I [12] .... bed at about half past nine.

Unit 5

1 **Complete the sentences with the correct form of the verbs in the brackets.**

1 Sarah _loves_ playing tennis. (love)
2 .... the phone! (answer)
3 George hates .... vegetables. (eat)
4 .... at this photo! (look)
5 .... your name here. (write)
6 They don't like .... to the cinema. (go)
7 Does she .... swimming? (like)
8 .... late for dinner! (not be)
9 We love .... football in the park. (play)
10 I like .... to music. (listen)

2 **Circle the correct words.**

1 .... you speak French?
   a **Can** b Does c Is
2 He can .... poetry.
   a writes b writing c write
3 Can he swim? Yes, he ....
   a can't b swim c can
4 .... hate going to restaurants.
   a He b She c They
5 Daniele .... his digital camera.
   a not can use b can't use c can't uses
6 My best friend loves .... magazines.
   a read b reading c reads
7 I hate .... early at the weekend.
   a to get up b geting up c getting up
8 Our dog .... football.
   a can play b can he play c can plays
9 Usman can do gymnastics ....
   a very well b very good c very nice
10 .... download music? Yes, I can.
   a You can b Do you can c Can you

3 ⊙ **2.37 Listen and complete the text.**

There's a sports competition at my school and my team is brilliant! All my friends can ¹ _play_ football quite well. They can all run ² .... , too. Molly can ³ .... gymnastics very well and Eddie can ⁴ .... Anna can do karate, and she can ⁵ .... volleyball, too. But I hate ⁶ .... I ⁷ .... football or volleyball. I can't do gymnastics ⁸ .... and I hate ⁹ .... But I can ¹⁰ .... text messages. Is that a sport?

Unit 6

1 **Find the mistakes and rewrite the correct sentences.**

1 What does you do on Saturday?
   What do you do on Saturday?
2 He goes usually home at half past three.
3 Where do she have lunch?
4 They do their homework always on Sunday night.
5 What time you get up?
6 I play computer games not often.
7 Where does he lives?
8 I go sometimes to the park after school.

2 **Circle the correct words**

1 Federica never .... her lunch at school.
   a **eats** b eat c eating
2 This is .... new bicycle.
   a my b me c mine
3 You mustn't .... this window.
   a not open b opening c open
4 We're going home. Come with ....
   a we b us c our
5 They .... their pets to school.
   a mustn't to take b don't must take
   c mustn't take
6 I get up .... half past six.
   a on b at c in
7 Do you like pizza? Yes, I ....
   a do b come c am
8 They go swimming .... Sunday.
   a at b on c in
9 She .... a life-jacket on the boat.
   a must wear b must wearing c do wear
10 .... does your mother work?
   a Where b What c Whose

3 ⊙ **2.50 Listen and complete the text.**

My name's Oliver and I ¹ _live_ in Liverpool. I go ² .... Newton Secondary School. It's a big school with about ³ .... students. We ⁴ .... lots of different subjects and the teachers are fun. I ⁵ .... Science and Art. I ⁶ .... my new school and I've got lots of new friends. I ⁷ .... have lunch with my best friend. He ⁸ .... computers. We sometimes ⁹ .... the web in the computer room ¹⁰ .... lunch.

Unit 7

1 Complete the conversation with *is*, *are*, *isn't*, *any*, *some* or *a*.

Mum is at the supermarket. She phones Dylan for help ...

Mum: Dylan. Can you look in the fridge, please? Is there ¹ any_____ milk?

Dylan: No, there ² _____ .

Mum: ³ _____ there any vegetables?

Dylan: Yes, there are ⁴ _____ carrots. And there ⁵ _____ some tomatoes.

Mum: ⁶ _____ there any fruit?

Dylan: There are ⁷ _____ apples and there's ⁸ _____ banana.

Mum: Are there any eggs?

Dylan: Yes, there ⁹ _____ . There are six eggs, but we haven't got ¹⁰ _____ ice cream, Mum!

2 (Circle) the correct words.

1 I've got _____ sweets.
   a many　**b** (lots of)　**c** much

2 How _____ chairs are there?
   a many　**b** lots of　**c** much

3 How _____ water is in the bottle?
   a many　**b** not much　**c** much

4 I haven't got _____ ideas for my project.
   a many　**b** not many　**c** much

5 Have you got _____ comics?
   a many　**b** not many　**c** much

6 There _____ much information about the museum.
   a aren't　**b** not　**c** isn't

3 ⊙ **3.06** **Listen and complete the text.**

My name's Stefano. I have coffee and milk with ¹ some_____ biscuits for breakfast. Then I have a sandwich or ² _____ crisps in the morning break. I have lunch at school. I always have ³ _____ of pasta! Then I usually have some ⁴ _____ or fish. In the afternoon I have a ⁵ _____ at home. At about 7.30, I have dinner with my family. We have ⁶ _____ meat, fish or cheese.

Unit 8

1 Complete the conversation with the correct form of the present continuous of the verb in the brackets.

1 **A** Are_____ you watching_____ the football match on TV? (watch)
   B No, I'm not_____ .

2 **A** What _____ you _____ ? (do)
   B I _____ an email. (write)

3 **A** Look. It _____ . Let's play tennis. (not rain)
   B Good idea.

4 **A** _____ David _____ his English homework? (do)
   B No, he _____ a comic. (read)

2 (Circle) the correct words.

1 I _____ my new trainers today.
   a wear　**b** ('m wearing)

2 Abena is in her bedroom. She _____ to music.
   a 's listening　**b** listens

3 Filippo _____ football at the weekends.
   a is playing　**b** plays

4 My brother _____ for his girlfriend. She's late!
   a is waiting　**b** waits

5 Edona's very musical. She _____ the piano and the guitar.
   a plays　**b** is playing

6 My friends _____ to school by bus every day.
   a are going　**b** go

3 ⊙ **3.16** **Listen and complete the text.**

It's Thursday and I usually ¹ go_____ to school, but today we are ² _____ Cambridge on a school trip. I love Cambridge and ³ _____ having a great time. Now it's one o'clock and it's lunchtime. We usually ⁴ _____ dinner at school in the canteen, but today we're ⁵ _____ here in a beautiful park. ⁶ _____ eating a sandwich and drinking orange juice. I'm ⁷ _____ a guide to Cambridge. My friend Daniele ⁸ _____ eating and he's sending a text message, too. Some of my friends ⁹ _____ sitting down. ¹⁰ _____ playing football.

Unit 9

1 **Complete the sentences with the correct form of the past simple of the verb *be*.**

1 We _were_ on holiday last week. (✓)
2 Peter _wasn't_ scared. (✗)
3 _____ you at school on Monday?
4 The students _____ in classroom 3. (✗)
5 Last week _____ cold and rainy. (✓)
6 Where _____ you yesterday morning?
7 _____ your brother at the football match yesterday?
8 My books _____ in my school bag. (✗)
9 _____ Jenny ill yesterday?

2 **Choose the correct verb.**

1 We _____ a DVD last night.
   a played   **b** ate   **c** watched
2 I _____ at home on Saturday.
   a stayed   **b** walked   **c** listened
3 We _____ to the cinema.
   a walked   **b** visited   **c** worked
4 I _____ my room at the weekend.
   a arrived   **b** tidied   **c** talked
5 The clock _____ at five o'clock.
   a studied   **b** phoned   **c** stopped

3 **Put the words in order to make sentences.**

1 for stayed Jake in hours two museum the
2 room to Max music listened his in
3 arrived twenty late my train minutes
4 aunt visited week in my Oxford last we
5 night in they band played the school last

4 ◉ **3.29** **Listen and complete the text.**

I'm Joe and I'm twelve years old. ¹_____ from New York in the United States. Last weekend I ²_____ my grandparents in Long Island. They ³_____ in New York when they ⁴_____ young. But now they ⁵_____ in a quiet place. I ⁶_____ my visit. We ⁷_____ hamburgers together in the garden. We ⁸_____ to the park and ⁹_____ a football match. In the evening we ¹⁰_____ a funny film on DVD, and Gran and Grampa ¹¹_____ me a video of their trip to Europe. And we ¹²_____ lots of games, but not computer games!

Unit 10

1 **Complete the sentences with the correct forms.**

1 My sister has _got_ a new bicycle.
   a have got   **b** has got   **c** got
2 William _____ computer games in the evening.
   a play   **b** playing   **c** plays
3 Isabel _____ to school.
   a don't walk   **b** not walk   **c** doesn't walk
4 What are you _____ on Sunday night?
   a doing   **b** do   **c** does
5 Why is the radio on? _____ there's a football match.
   a Why   **b** Because   **c** Then
6 She _____ sweets.
   a must eat not   **b** mustn't eats
   c mustn't eat
7 They _____ in Paris in 2008.
   a live   **b** lived   **c** lives
8 _____ playing tennis with Ben tomorrow afternoon.
   a I'm   **b** Am   **c** I do
9 _____ juggle three balls?
   a Do you can   **b** Can you   **c** You can
10 _____ they at home last night?
   a Was   **b** Were   **c** Are

2 ◉ **3.42** **Listen and complete the text with one word in each gap.**

My name's Emma and I'm from London. I've ¹_____ two brothers and a sister. I like computers, but I ²_____ like sport. At the moment I'm ³_____ this email and I'm ⁴_____ to music.
I ⁵_____ cycle to school because it ⁶_____ near my house. I ⁷_____ by bus with my sister. We ⁸_____ lunch at school and we get home at 4 o'clock.
On Saturday I often ⁹_____ shopping. On Sunday I usually ¹⁰_____ my gran. Last Sunday, my brothers and I ¹¹_____ her in the kitchen. We ¹²_____ a fantastic lunch.
Tomorrow is Monday – the first day of the holidays. I'm ¹³_____ my friends in the city centre. But we ¹⁴_____ going shopping. We're ¹⁵_____ a picnic in the park.

Your Space

Web Zone

http://yourspace.cambridge.org

Your Space DVD

Featuring:

Video diaries

Viewpoints

Communication

Culture

CLIL

Thanks and Acknowledgements

The authors and publishers would like to thank the teachers who commented on the material at different stages of its development, the teachers who allowed us to observe their classes, and those who gave up their valuable time for interviews and focus groups. Unfortunately, space does not allow us to mention these people individually by name.

The authors would like to thank all the people who have worked so hard on *Your Space*. We are especially grateful to James Dingle for inviting us to write this project and for his support during all stages of its development. We would also like to thank Frances Amrani, commissioning editor, and the editors Claire Powell, Rosemary Bradley and Ruth Bell-Pellegrini for their skilled editorial contributions, perceptive editing, and commitment to the project; the design team at Wild Apple; David Lawton for his design ideas; Emma Szlachta for her excellent project management and Graham Avery, production manager for his support. We are grateful to all the other writers on the project for their creative input. We would also like to thank the many reviewers and teachers who contributed to the development of this course. We extend a special thank you to the editor Rachael Gibbons for her unwavering focus during the development process.

The publishers acknowledge the following sources of copyright material and are grateful for the permissions granted. While every effort has been made, it has not always been possible to identify the sources of all the material used, or to trace all copyright holders. If any omissions are brought to our notice, we will be happy to include the appropriate acknowledgements on reprinting.

Photo Acknowledgements

p. 9 (1, 6, 9 & 10): Thinkstock; p. 9 (2): Thinkstock/Stockbyte; p. 9 (3): Shutterstock/Lasse Kristensen; p. 9 (4): Thinkstock/Jupiterimages; p. 9 (5): Thinkstock/Ryan McVay; p. 9 (7): Shutterstock/Venus Angel; p. 9 (9): Shutterstock/PRIMA; p. 13: Thinkstock/Goodshoot; p. 15 (L): Shutterstock/Katrina Brown; p. 15 ®: imagebroker/Alamy; p. 16 (6): Shutterstock/Peter Zurek; p. 16 (BL & BC), 21 (L) and 40: Shutterstock/Monkey Business Images; p. 16 (BR): Shutterstock/AVAVA; p. 19 (TL): Courtesy of Martyn Townsend; p. 19 (TC): Shutterstock/Morgan Lane Photography; p. 19 (C): Shutterstock/Anna Halkouskaya; p. 19 (BC): Shutterstock/MalibuBooks; p. 19 (TR): Lucidio Studio Inc./Corbis; p. 19 (CR): Kris Mercer/Alamy; p. 19 (BR): Shutterstock/David Hughes; p. 20: iStock/© digitalskillet; p. 21 ®: iStock/© Leigh Schindler; p.24 Shutterstock/Mandy Godbehear; p. 41 (5): Shutterstock/Klaus Kaulitzki; p. 27 (L): Courtesy of Zoe Vardi; p. 27 (R): Robie Chowdbury; p. 30 (L): iStock/© Joshua Hodge Photography; p. 30 (R): iStock/© Ana Abejon; p. 35: © Alex Segre/Alamy; p. 36 (TL): Sandra Ford Photography; p. 36 (TL): Jon Durrant/Alamy; p. 36 (CL: B Christopher/Alamy; p. 36 (CR): Adam Woolfitt/CORBIS; p. 36 (BL): Life File Photo Library Ltd/Alamy; p. 36 (BR): Courtesy of Robbie Escater; p. 37 (T): Courtesy of Emma Hall; p. 37 (B): Courtesy of Nazim Khan; p. 39 (T/Inset & BC): Shutterstock/Leah-Anne Thompson; p. 39 (T/main): Shutterstock/Leah-Anne Thompson; p. 39 (Pete): Shutterstock/Lisa F. Young; p. 39 (Jenny): Grain Belt Pictures/Alamy; p. 39 (Kevin): Shutterstock/Stacy Barnett; p. 39 (Helen): A ROOM WITH VIEWS / Alamy; p. 39 (Jo): Blaine Harrington III/Alamy; p. 39 (John): ACE STOCK LIMITED/Alamy; p. 39 (Claire): Caro/Alamy; p. 39 (Rob): Ben Molyneux People/Alamy; p. 39 (Sarah): vario images GmbH & Co.KG/Alamy; p. 39 (Tim): Shutterstock/Lisa F. Young; p. 39 (Tom): Angela Hampton Picture Library/Alamy; p. 39 (Oliver): Davide Piras/Alamy; p. 39 (Chloe): Ted Horowitz/Alamy; p. 39 (Ben): JJM Stock Photography/Commercial/Alamy; p. 39 (Nick): WoodyStock/Alamy; p. 39 (Jessica): Horizon International Images Limited/Alamy; p. 41 (1, 3 & 4): Thinkstock; p. 41 (2): Shutterstock/Callahan; p. 41 (3): pp. 41 (5): Shutterstock/Klaus Kaulitzki ; p. 41 (6): © moodboard/SuperStock; p. 41 (7): Shutterstock/maxstockphoto; p. 41 (8): Thinkstock/Ablestock.com; p. 50: iStock/© Joshua Hodge Photography; p. 54: Shutterstock/Sonya Etchison; p.56(L): Corbis/Neal Preston; p. 56(T): Getty Images/Andreas Kindler; p. 56(R): Alamy/Bill Bachman; p. 57(T1): alamy/Gary Roebuck; p. 57(T2): Shutterstock/Nicholas Sutcliffe; 57(T3): Shutterstock/AVAVA; p57(T4): Shutterstock/Yuri Arcurs; p.57(T5): Shutterstock/Lorraine Swanson; p.57(B1): Alamy/Ilian Stage: p 57(B2): Shutterstock/Sudheer Sakthan; p57(B3): Shutterstock/Laurence Gough; p. 57(B4): Shutterstock/Jeff Dalton; p. 57(B5): Shutterstock/Michaeljung; p. 60: © PhotoAlto / Alamy; p. 61(T): Shutterstock/prodakszyn; p. 61(B): Shutterstock/Galina Barskaya; p. 64 (T): © Amana Images INC./Alamy; p. 64 (UC): Shutterstock/Kruchankova; Maya; p. 64 (BC): iStock/© zorani; p. 64 (B): © PhotosIndia.com LLC/Alamy; p. 66: Alamy/Ian Shaw; p.67 (CR): Shutterstock/Dhoxax; p. 67 (TL): Shutterstock/photoaloja; p. 67 (CB): Shutterstock/dennis Donohue; p. 75 (CFR): shutterstock/Jill Lang; p67 (CL): Shutterstock/Peter Hansen; p. 67 (BL) Shutterstock/Eric Gevaerrt; p.67 (TR): Shutterstock/Ivan Histand; p. 67 (BR): Shutterstock/Chris Fourie; p. 69 (T): Getty Images/Altrendo Image; p. 69 (BL): iStock/Kelly Cline; p. 69 (BC): Getty Images/Peter Cade; p. 69 (BR): © MBI/Alamy; p. 71 (TR): © image100/SuperStock; p. 71 (BL): Shutterstock/Magone; p. 74: © Photofusion Picture Library/Alamy; p. 77 (2): © MBI/Alamy; p. 77 (3 & 6): educationphotos.co.uk/walmsley; p. 88 (1): 1Apix / Alamy; p. 88 (2): Juniors Bildarchiv/Alamy; p. 88 (3): Tim Davis/Corbis; p. 88 (4): H Lansdown/Alamy; p. 88 (5): SCPhotos/Alamy; p. 88 (6): PCL / Alamy; p. 88 (7): blickwinkel/Alamy; p. 88 (8): Juniors Bildarchiv/Alamy; p. 89 (TL): Alton Towers; p. 89 (TC): Getty Images/Getty Images; p. 89 (TR): Stuart Crump/Alamy; p. 89 (BR): Atlantide Phototravel/Corbis; p. 91: © Yuri Arcurs/Alamy; p. 87 (1): Shutterstock/Joe Gough; p. 87 (2): Shutterstock/Daniel Padavona; p. 87 (3): Shutterstock/WITTY234; p. 87 (4): Shutterstock/Ruth Black; p.87 (5): Shutterstock/Viktar Malyshchyts and Shutterstock/Rafa Irusta; p. 87 (6): Shutterstock/Kheng Guan Toh; p. 87 (7): Shutterstock/Joe Gough; p87 (8): Shutterstock/Elena Elisseeva; p. 94 (Henry): Getty Images/Jonathan Knowles; p. 94 (Alice): Shutterstock/Monkey Business Images; p. 94 (Alex): Shutterstock/jackhollingsworthcom, LLC; p. 94 (Julia): Shutterstock/paulaphoto; p. 94 (Jade): iStock/© blackwaterimages; p. 97 (L): PHIL NOBLE/Reuters/Corbis; p. 97 (TC): Robert Harding Picture Library Ltd/Alamy; p. 97 (BC): Kevin Britland/Alamy; p. 97 (R): PBstock/Alamy; p. 99 (C): © Brave Rabbit; p99 (BR): ©Ian Dagnall / Alamy; p. 99 (BL): Nikuwka/Shutterstock; p. 100: Shutterstock; p. 99 (BR): © Howard Barlow / Alamy; p. 101 (T): Shutterstock/Monkey Business Images; p. 101 (UC): iStock/© PaulSimcock; p. 101 (BC): iStock/© Joshua Hodge Photography; p. 101 (B): iStock/© Aldo Murillo; p. 103: PA News; p. 103 (B/G): Shutterstock/Yurico; p. 104: © GlowImages/Alamy; p. 105: wavebreakmedia ltd; p. 107 (BCR): RIA NOVOSTI / SCIENCE PHOTO LIBRARY; p. 107 (TCR): © CORBIS; p. 107 (carpet): Shutterstock/Martin Trajkovski ; p. 107 (clock): Shutterstock/Sashkin ; p. 107 (coffee beans): Shutterstock/Valentyn Volkov; p. 107 (toothbrush): Shutterstock/Paul Matthew Photography; p. 107 (chess set): Shutterstock/Mike Flippo; p. 107 (camera): Shutterstock/3355m; p. 107 (pasta): Shutterstock/cappi Thompson; p. 107 (umbrella): Shutterstock/Excellent backgrounds HERE; p. 107 (tea): iStock/© Sara Sanger; p. 110: © Steve Vidler / SuperStock; p. 112 (BL): Shutterstock/Elena Elisseeva; p. 112 (TR): Sunflowers, 1888 (oil on canvas), Gogh, Vincent van (1853-90) / National Gallery, London, UK / The Bridgeman Art Library; p. 113 (flag): Shutterstock/Alexander Gatsenko; p. 113 (sign): Shutterstock/More Similar Images; p. 113 (felucca): Shutterstock/Jeffrey Liao; p. 113 (juggling): © Johner Images / Alamy; p. 113 (Empire State Building): Shutterstock/akva; p. 113 (Tutankhamen): © The Gallery Collection/Corbis; p. 113 (goldfish): Shutterstock/Tischenko Irina; p. 114 (1): Shutterstock/Alex Staroseltsev; p. 114 (2): Shutterstock/MaszaS; p. 114 (3): Shutterstock/Dimitry Kalinovsky; p. 114 (4): Shutterstock/hamurishi; p. 114 (5): Shutterstock/Serp; p. 114 (6): Shutterstock/Elena elisseeva; p. 114 (7): Shutterstock/Phase4Photography; p. 114 (8): © Design Pics Inc./Alamy; p. 115 (Fred, Lucas & Tilly): Shutterstock/Monkey Business Images; p. 115 (Erin): iStock/© gisele; p. 115 (Molly): Shutterstock/Eric Wagner; p. 116 (BC): © Chip Simons/Science Faction/Corbis; p. 116 (T): © VO TRUNG DUNG/CORBIS SYGMA; p. 116 © Bettmann/CORBIS.

Commissioned photos by Gareth Boden for pages 8, 10, 11, 17, 23, 29 (photos A-D), 43, 53, 73, 79, 93, 99 (TL) and 109.

Artwork Acknowledgements

Rob McKlurkan p. 10, 12B, 27; Dusan Pavlic (*Beehive Illustration*) p. 12T, 46T, 47, 72; David Benham (*Graham Cameron Illustration*) p. 13, 34B, 82, 86, 96; Nick Kobyluch p. 14; Jake Lawrence p. 20, 24, 30, 31, 34T, 40, 44T, 50, 51, 54, 60, 64, 70, 74T, 80, 84L, 90L, 94, 100, 104, 110; Adrian Barclay (*Beehive Illustration*) p. 21, 28, 46B, 68; Matt Ward (*Beehive Illustration*) p. 22, 48, 76, 102; Ned Woodman p. 25, 35, 45, 55, 65R, 75, 85R, 95R, 105, 115; Andy Parker p. 26, 33, 49; Army of Trolls p. 32; Mark Ruffle p. 41, 58, 65L, 74B; Andrew Hennessey p. 42, 46, 61; Sean Longcroft (*Art Collection*) p. 44B, 78, 92, 101, 111, 112, 113; David Semple p. 63; Richard Pashley p. 81L/R, 84R, 85L, 91; Humberto Blanco (*Sylvie Poggio*) p. 90R, 95L; Mike Lacey (*Beehive Illustration*) p. 106, 116; Simon Rumble (*Beehive Illustration*) p. 117T; Carl Pearce p. 118, 119, 120 ,121, 123, 124, 125T, 126, 127; Martin Sanders p. 125B; Kevin Hopgood p. 129, 130,131, 132, 133, 134, 135, 136, 137

Cover concept design by Andrew Oliver

The publishers would like to extend a warm thanks to all the teachers and freelance collaborators who have made a valuable contribution to this material.